LIGHT
your
LANTERN

JOSHY THOMAS

INDIA • SINGAPORE • MALAYSIA

Copyright © Joshy Thomas 2023
All Rights Reserved.

ISBN 979-8-89066-822-6

This book has been published with all efforts taken to make the material error-free after the consent of the author. However, the author and the publisher do not assume and hereby disclaim any liability to any party for any loss, damage, or disruption caused by errors or omissions, whether such errors or omissions result from negligence, accident, or any other cause.

While every effort has been made to avoid any mistake or omission, this publication is being sold on the condition and understanding that neither the author nor the publishers or printers would be liable in any manner to any person by reason of any mistake or omission in this publication or for any action taken or omitted to be taken or advice rendered or accepted on the basis of this work. For any defect in printing or binding the publishers will be liable only to replace the defective copy by another copy of this work then available.

Dedication

I am deeply grateful
to my teachers, mentors and spiritual masters
to my companions, confreres and colleagues
to my batch mates, seniors and juniors
to my friends and well-wishers
known as the 'Salesians of Don Bosco.'

Appreciation for 'Light Your Lantern'

Joshy's work is an affirmation of faith in the power of finer, exemplary human qualities demonstrable via our competencies, capabilities and character, being directed for the greater good. He points to the need and possibility of realizing a purposive, progressive, prosperous and peaceful world for one and all.

Prof. Dr. LS Ganesh

Vice Chancellor
ICFAI Foundation for Higher Education
Professor (retd)
Department of Management Studies, IIT Madras

Post COVID 19, the VUCA world has assumed greater significance and people are grappling to reboot themselves. This book is coming out at the most opportune time, wherein people not only need to light their lantern but also of the people around them.

This book indeed makes a very sincere attempt to give a comprehensive toolkit to the readers to "Earn

Confidence". A must-read book for people who want to fight mediocrity and achieve greater significance in life.

Mohit Gandhi

Principal Advisor
Prin.L.N.Welingkar Institute of Management
Development & Research

I congratulate Joshy Thomas, first 'Salt and Light' and now 'Light your Lantern'.

To remove the darkness, light a candle…to live a brighter life, read the book, 'Light your Lantern'. I appreciate the way the author brings an amazing perspective to everyday life so that we may live joyfully. May God bless his endeavours!

Vijay Michihito Batra

Motivational Speaker, Life Coach, Author

We are in a VUCA world. We need the strength, confidence and courage to face the challenges in our day-to-day life, both personal and professional.

This book is focused on guiding you on the techniques to improve your confidence level, strength, skill and positive attitude. The great news is that this will work for anyone.

Joshy has written practically and elegantly so that every reader can illuminate positivity.

Dr. Ravi Veeraraghavan

Officiating Director, Xavier Institute of Management & Entrepreneurship, Chennai

Leadership is the ability of an individual or a group of individuals to influence and guide followers. The success of an undertaking depends on the quality of leadership and hence, it has become an indispensable facet of modern society. Although it is something innate, it is possible for people to be trained in leadership. This explains the large quantity of literature that has flooded the market in recent times on leadership in order to help the aspiring youth to be trained in taking up management roles in their respective areas of interest.

'Light your Lantern' contains various facets of leadership. The title of the book is based on the words of Jesus Christ: "You are the Light of the World" (Mt 5:14). His leadership style was characterized by compassion, love, and servanthood. Jesus was not only a servant-leader but also a good shepherd who was ready to die for his people. The idea of leading others begins in the heart which leads to pleasing the heart of God.

Genuine leaders must become lights and radiate positivity through their thoughts, words and deeds. Ignorance is darkness and it makes one biased, intolerant, impulsive and truthless. People who live in such darkness can never be good leaders. On the other hand, light is wisdom. The possessors of light become unbiased, positive, confident and enlightened. They are contented, happy and are destined to become great leaders.

The book is made up of four sections and each of these has a number of chapters dealing with different aspects of leadership. Joshy Thomas through various imageries and wholesome examples takes the readers to the world of transformational leadership that can help in building up a society that is just, peaceful and prosperous.

While congratulating the author for this innovative approach to leadership, I invite the readers to delve deeply into the sea of information contained in the book that can enable us to become worthy leaders in our fragile world of today.

Dr. George Rajendran

Bishop of Tucklay, Tamil Nadu

'Light Your Lantern' by Joshy Thomas promises to be an engaging narrative for many of us on managing life more than just being a manager for life! He is firm and friendly, frank and free in his simple storytelling style. The chapter, 'Learn More to Grow More', sums up the writer's beliefs in a nutshell.

The passion to reach out and transform is very palpable in an endearing way to readers' hearts!

Keshav M

CEO Mantra & Founder Director
Chennai Chapter L&D Global

Joshy Thomas is a committed professional who strives to bring value to those he works with. Through this book, he shares with a wider audience his own experiences and thoughts on the new challenges faced by managers today, how to balance the demands of a dynamic and increasingly digital workplace with empathy and a humane approach and how to make one's inner light shine.

Young entrants in the corporate sector as well as seasoned professionals will get new insights from this book.

Prof. Smeeta Bhatkal

Dean, Banking, Financial Services & Insurance
Prin.L.N.Welingkar Institute of Management
Development & Research

My heartfelt appreciation to Joshy Thomas for this insightful journey into our life and into our minds through 'Light Your Lantern'. The book is a treat to read. It exhorts us to light the lantern we are born with and also to light the lanterns of others to handle the unprecedented challenges in our personal and professional life.

The four strands of the lantern is an innovative, classic idea – because it progresses from attitude to skill to lighting the lantern of others and finally becoming the LIGHT itself. Wow!!

Dr. J Henry Rozario

Corporate Trainer & Leadership Coach
Exodus Consulting

I am glad to know that Joshy Thomas has written a sequel to his book 'Salt and Light: A Leader on a Pilgrimage'.

His first book was a delight to read and I had recommended it as a 'must read' book to my students of management courses in institutes with which I am associated as faculty. In that book, he had elucidated many aspects that are essential for everyone especially those at the start of their leadership journey.

I am sure Joshy has expanded on the themes in his new book, "Light Your Lantern". I had an opportunity, courtesy to the author, to have a preview of the new book. I got an inkling that a few of the chapters in his new book would light the lanterns of the readers.

I look forward eagerly to hold the book in my hands, tuck into a cosy corner and read it from beginning to end as early as possible.

Dr. R Ravi Sankar

Professor, Indus Business Academy, Bengaluru

'Light Your Lantern' is the perfect gift for every new-age professional. It is a collection of wisdom that has the power to build life, shape dreams and design career. The reader is exhorted to become a value-driven professional for the present and the future world of turbulence.

Bindu Jose

Headmistress, Govt. HSS, Balal

"Everyone is born with a lantern. The wise have it lit, while the ignorant hold it unlit and live in darkness. It is a mandate for those with light to share the light."

This quote from the book, most certainly resonates with me. Yes, everyone is truly born with a lantern. What we choose to do with it, is what shapes who we are, and become. Those with the light, must consciously and wisely choose the path of giving and sharing.

I am sparked with curiosity to read more coming up in the following chapters -

- Give Your Best to be the Best

- The Corporate Monks

The previous book. 'Salt and Light' was wonderful. This one, will do wonders! My compliments and best wishes to Joshy Thomas.

Paayal Varma

Head - Customer Solutions, Dale Carnegie of India

For the last two years, nights became longer and weekends became shorter; I saw the author, persistently and passionately carving out a masterpiece mostly based on his experience. 'Salt and Light' gave hope. 'Light Your Lantern' will illuminate the world better. Let the Light Shine!

Prof. Dr. Thomas Rosy

Dean, International Programs
& Prof. Mathematics, Madras Christian College

'Light Your Lantern' by Joshy Thomas is a must read book for every visionary leader who is on a mission to transform the world by spreading light. The author uses the image of a lantern and its wicks to elucidate powerful reflections and thus offers an all-round wellbeing and abundance to the readers.

The book will expose your strengths and leadership potential and will give you immense insights to face the storms of life.

Dr. John Parankimalil

Executive Director
Don Bosco Institute of Management, Guwahati

Contents

The Path to Immortality

The Light of Life

Acknowledgement

Every being, including humans, illuminates the world through good acts. Even a tiny firefly makes its sincere effort to light up the world. Likewise, 'Light Your Lantern' is my humble commitment to spread the light.

'Salt and Light: A Leader on a Pilgrimage' was born in 2020. I dreamt and fantasized how it looked in the hands of readers. I dreamt of people quoting from it and writing its reviews.

Thoughts become things! Some dreams become real, if we dream with passion.

I was extremely delighted by the response I received after the publication of 'Salt and Light'. Readers filled the social media with reviews and comments; reviewers like Silverfish broadcasted it on YouTube; professors and teachers suggested the book to their students and stored their libraries with copies; leadership coaches and trainers curated programs based on its contents; spiritual men and women began to read it for their spiritual reflections; professionals used it as a self-development tool or as a precious gift for a beloved friend.

Everyone appreciated its simplicity and profoundness. They benefitted from its soul-searching reflections, got inspired by its thought-provoking stories and were transformed by the pilgrimage.

I am deeply grateful to these readers and well-wishers for their positive feedback, words of appreciation and for the suggestions they gave to improve the book.

Soon they began to enquire about a sequence to 'Salt and Light'. They gently pushed and urged me not to stop making a difference. They encouraged me to come up with another book. 'Light Your Lantern' is the fruit of their persistence.

I should admit that like 'Salt and Light', there is nothing new and nothing unknown in this book too!

All insights flow from familiar fountains but take the reader to new shores. There are no surprises; no innovative ideas or out-of-the box theories. It doesn't contain any supernatural experiences or divine revelations; I never had one! It elucidates some common thoughts from a common man. It aims to spread a humble ray of light like the tiny fireflies.

God, the Divine Light, has always been my inspiration and the source of strength. I thank God for filling my life with light and for the gift of lovely people who radiate my life with love and joy.

I would like to thank all those who inspired me to pursue this dream and nurtured my passion to reach this marvelous day. I thank my beloved parents whose love, support and care led me all through my life. My wife, Dr. Thomas Rosy, meticulously read the manuscript with a scientist's mind and has always been by my side with encouraging support and love. Her enthusiasm acted as a catalyst to complete this work and she suggested the title 'Light Your Lantern'. I thank my family for their love and affection that motivated me in this adventurous journey.

'Light Your Lantern' has become richer and immensely profound with the insightful foreword by Dr. Oliver S. Crocco, Assistant Professor, School of Leadership & Human Resource Development, Louisiana State University. As one of the foremost visionaries of Gamification in Learning, he has influenced organizations to reduce the mindless monotony at work by gamifying certain functions. I thank him for adding depth and value to this book. I thank my friend Dr. Nibu Thomas, Department of Management Studies, IIT Madras, for linking me to Dr. Oliver.

Dr. John Parankimalil, Executive Director, Don Bosco Institute of Management, Guwahati, my teacher and superior, has been a constant source of inspiration and encouragement for nearly three decades. While designing my trainings, I freely pick up quotes, insights and anecdotes from his numerous books and videos. I have done it in this book too.

When in darkness, I had the fortune to reach out to legendary leaders like Fr. VM Thomas, an MBA from Harvard and Founder Director, DBI, Guwahati. While working with him, he taught me the foundations of HRD and lighted up my days through his daily mentoring. I am grateful to him for the encouraging guidance he gives me daily. The values I gained from him appear in this book on almost every chapter. Like 'Salt and Light', 'Light Your Lantern' too owes much to his guidance.

My friends Dr. George Rajendran, Bishop of Tucklay, Tamil Nadu and Shajan Varghese, Principal Consultant, Ganistom, supported and inspired me in many ways to get this work completed. Thanks to both of you.

Yashwant Shrivastav R, a highly talented and budding Finance professional, thoughtfully captured the concepts through cartoons and patiently spent hours to make the book aesthetically marvelous. I am deeply grateful to him for the creative support.

I am blessed and enriched by the endorsements of renowned leaders like Dr. Prof. MJ Xavier, Chair, Centre for Technology & Innovation, LIBA Chennai and Founder Director, IIM Ranchi; Prof. LS Ganesh, Vice Chancellor, ICFAI Foundation for Higher Education and Professor (retd), Department of Management Studies, IIT Madras; Mr. Mohit Gandhi, Principal Advisor, Prin.L.N.Welingkar Institute of Management Development & Research; Mr. Vijay Michihito Batra, Motivational Speaker, Life Coach and Author; Dr. Ravi Veeraraghavan, Officiating Director, Xavier Institute of Management & Entrepreneurship, Chennai; Mr. Keshav M, CEO Mantra & Founder Director, Chennai Chapter L&D Global; Prof. Smeeta Bhatkal, Dean, Banking, Financial Services &

Insurance, Prin.L.N.Welingkar Institute of Management Development & Research; Dr. J Henry Rozario, Corporate Trainer & Leadership Coach, Exodus Consulting; Dr. R Ravi Sankar, Professor, Indus Business Academy, Bengaluru; Ms Bindu Jose, Headmistress, Govt. HSS, Balal; Ms Paayal Varma, Head, Customer Solutions, Dale Carnegie of India.

Thank you for lighting my lantern!

I thank Sweta and Mydhili from Notion Press for their immense help in the making of this book.

Words are not sufficient to express my gratitude to the participants of my training programs. I had the opportunity to learn from over 55,000 participants in the last 22 years. They touched my life. This book contains some of those insights and reflections they taught me.

Finally as I dedicate this book to the Salesians of Don Bosco, I would like to express my sincere and humble gratitude to all those wonderful friends, and confreres who stood by me and helped me to reach what I am today.

Life had its ups and downs with glories and sorrows. It had good days and not so good days. However, in the rough ocean of life, they were like a lighthouse, helping me to sail on looking to the Light!

I wish and pray that we become light to brighten this world.

Light Your Lantern. Let it shine!

Foreword

'Light Your Lantern,' is an insightful guide for those who aspire to grow in their career and become effective leaders. The book takes inspiration from the words of the Christian exemplar Jesus Christ, who said to his followers, 'You are the Light of the World.' True to its title, the book encourages readers to add light and positivity through their actions, words and mindsets.

While written from a Christian perspective, this book will appeal to people of different religious traditions or those from none because it focuses on universally shared principles of light, truth and goodness. Joshy's previous work, 'Salt and Light: A Leader on a Pilgrimage,' was aimed specifically at leaders; 'Light Your Lantern' is for everyone who seeks to use their unique gifts to illuminate the world joyfully.

I got to know Joshy Thomas through our mutual friend, Dr. Nibu John Thomas, with whom I have been working on Human Resource Development (HRD) research related to gamification since 2021. Gamification seeks to incorporate game-like attributes into typical work functions like training and performance management, to activate those same feelings of joy, fun and play in the workplace.

As someone who appreciates play and tries to avoid mindless monotony at work, it has been a passion of mine to focus on ways, workplaces can gamify certain functions. This relates to Joshy's book because ultimately magnifying light in the world brings much of the same positivity into the world. The author mentions 'fun' over 15 times and 'joy' over 30 times throughout the book!

When I teach my courses in the School of Leadership and Human Resource Development at Louisiana State University in the United States, I share at the beginning of class that everyone has something to contribute to our discussions because everyone has different work and life experiences, different worldviews or paradigms and different beliefs about the nature of reality.

We all have things to learn from one another. Even students brand new to the content have critical minds to question the embedded assumptions that many of us hold and that have been entrenched in our minds for many years. In this book, Joshy captures this idea by showing how everyone has a light they can use to support the thriving of others.

The book employs the metaphor of light, which is compelling for its relatedness to our lived experiences. When we walk, we need light to see the path in front of us. When we read, we need light to illuminate the pages. Humans use metaphors to help us make sense of our surroundings and share our meaning with others, which this book does very well with the metaphor of light.

It is important to note that light does not necessarily mean happiness. Research shows some people are predisposed to having higher levels of happiness depending on a variety of genetic and environmental conditions.

Those who experience darkness should not feel that it is somehow their fault or that they are hopeless. Rather, it is important to realize that there are things that they can do to build their happiness. One of these is intentionally reframing experiences in their lives through cognitive behavioural therapy or books like this that help to see things in new ways.

As a member of the Board of Directors of the Academy of Human Resource Development (www.ahrd.org) in the United States, I am particularly fond of the way the author speaks of the role of learning in cultivating light in oneself and one's organizations. In many ways, learning is a form of light that we can use to build on our knowledge and skills, shift our mindsets and potentially transform our meaning, perspectives or paradigms.

The world today is facing innumerable social, environmental, economic and political challenges that are compounding and growing in complexity. Technological advances, particularly in artificial intelligence, are transgressing previously assumed limits of human invention. In this book, the author rightfully questions whether advances in technology will make us more empathetic, humane, or kind. We will never be able to outsource those important human qualities.

As commonly stated, people have become the product of technology instead of its customers or primary intended users. We must always be wary of the influence and invasion of technology in our lives and we can never expect technology to replace our need to live lives full of light.

Joshy believes that ignorance is darkness, which can lead to hidden biases, narrow-mindedness, impulsiveness and truthlessness, which ultimately bring loneliness, isolation and groupthink. On the other hand, light represents wisdom, which leads to critical reflection on one's long-held assumptions, positivity, confidence, contentment and effectiveness in one's life and work.

To those fortunate enough to live in the light, we are responsible for spreading light among others, making the world a more joyful place to live and work.

Professionals who seek to develop their own light within themselves have the potential to be change agents who willingly serve amidst critical situations, look to the future with hope and build cohesive teams with high levels of integrity.

In 'Light Your Lantern,' Joshy Thomas provides readers with practical tools and guidance on how to become light and illuminate positivity through their lives. The book encourages individuals to take responsibility for lighting the lanterns of others, helping to dispel darkness and make the world a more habitable place.

It is an inspiring and insightful read for anyone aspiring to grow in career and become effective leader in today's uncertain times.

May the words in this book be a light to you and help you along the journey.

Dr. Oliver S. Crocco

Assistant Professor
School of Leadership and Human Resource
Development
Louisiana State University, USA

The Tiny Light from a Tiny Firefly!

The Sanskrit word 'Bharata' means 'Agni' or fire. Fire gives light, warmth, protection, happiness and hope. It also refers to those who dedicate their lives to become wise and virtuous by dispelling darkness and ignorance. Just as the fire purifies and even consumes darkness without getting corrupted, those with light purify the world through their virtuous life. They make the world better.

The inhabitants of 'Bharata' are the people of light. They spread the light by lighting the lanterns of others. Those with light are the seekers of the ultimate truth and they freely share the light with others. They love light! Light is a life-giving power!

Ignorance is darkness. It makes one biased, opinionated, impulsive and truthless. In fact, those in darkness live miserable lives. Light, on the other hand, is wisdom. The possessors of light become unbiased, positive, confident and enlightened. They are contented, happy and are destined to be prosperous. They dispel darkness through peace, charity and love.

The Holy Bible speaks of a world engulfed in total darkness in the beginning. God didn't like darkness; so

He said, "Let there be light!" Without light the universe was a wasteland. With light it became fertile and inhabitable. So as people of light, it is our responsibility to spread light and diminish darkness. We need to make the world habitable. We need to fill the world with light.

Everyone is born with a lantern. The wise have it lit and live in light while the ignorant hold it unlit and live in darkness. It is a mandate for those with light to share the light. At times we curse the darkness instead of lighting a lantern. At times we blame those who live in darkness without taking steps to light their lanterns. At times we prefer to stay aloof and away. At times we live in darkness though our lanterns are lit!

From 'Salt and Light' to 'Light Your Lantern'

Pole vault is a sport that displays a person's strength, speed, stamina and flexibility. The spectators on the gallery, the media, the sponsors and the government bestow accolades and praises on the pole-vaulter who uses a long and flexible pole to jump over a bar.

However, some vital things go unnoticed by everyone as they celebrate the victory. The pole itself; the cushion on which the pole-vaulter falls after the jump; the cross bar and even the coach. These are conveniently ignored.

While a good pole-vaulter will recognize the contribution of everyone and everything, most take them for granted. He knows that his performance is the result of the sincere efforts of everyone. Therefore he attributes his fame and success to the contributions of others.

I owe my heartfelt gratitude to all my readers and well-wishers for their appreciation and acceptance of my humble initiative. You inspired me to leap into a world of immense possibilities and positivity.

Overwhelmed by the affection and encouraging response I received for my first book 'Salt and Light: A Leader on a Pilgrimage', I ventured into my second book 'Light Your Lantern'. I thank all those who showered upon me their blessings of appreciation and gave me valuable suggestions. I am privileged to have amazing people like you as my friends and well-wishers.

If 'Salt and Light' was for the leaders, 'Light Your Lantern' is for everyone. This is my sincere attempt to light up my lantern! This is my humble gift to light up the world!

Our life is sprinkled with unprecedented challenges, personal and professional, health and financial, societal and family. But we exhibit courage and strength to brave the storm and walk ahead through the desert even in pitch darkness. We showcase our brilliance in every aspect of our lives. We always endeavour to do the right and the most important things in life. We play our unique and pivotal role to get this world back on track to drive ahead. We strive hard to bring progress and prosperity to everyone including us.

The world is surprisingly different from what it was a few years ago. Uncertainty is at an all-time high. We experience complete disruptions at our homes and workplaces. Though life span has increased the depth of relationship has decreased. We have material prosperity on one side and spiritual impoverishment on the other. Though physical distance among us has diminished with the arrival of internet, the emotional distance has become longer. We have become more capable but are incapable of managing ourselves. Our calibre is tested by numerous sudden turbulences.

Are we prepared for these turbulences?

There are rays of hope! For those who have their lanterns lit, it's an opportunity to expose their strengths and leadership capabilities. They gain immense insights into the tremors and turpitudes of life. They remind us that tough people last longer than tough times!

A New Gift for the New Age Professional

The new-age leader is a transformational change agent. He willingly takes charge of critical situations and complex challenges, looks to the future with hope and is even selfless while executing the strategy. He cares for the people with an egalitarian mind, builds cohesive teams and encourages transparency. He is a builder of a community of high performers with high integrity.

Technology is invading every area of our life today. Does this technological revolution have a heart? Is it making us more empathetic, humane and kind? There is a rush to make everyone techno-savvy. Are we losing our people-savvy mindset in this mad rush?

Our digital tools and analytics help us to forecast potential disruptions with precision. Are we able to forecast the feelings of people? Is our confidence getting ruptured by the massive onslaught of digital revolutions? Is it empowering us to become more humane and humble?

While our work and life get reshaped by digital advancements, we must also redesign our thoughts, attitudes and behaviours to adapt to the present day life. We should have the heart to light a lantern.

Of course, we should be champions of this digital change and must keep pace with the challenges by acquiring a new set of competencies. Confidence doesn't come from 'being in control'. It comes from our humble admission that 'we don't control everything'. This is the vulnerability that we all need today to grow up with.

Can we discover once again the curiosity that we lost somewhere in life? Can we go back to our childhood days and rediscover that curiosity when we would challenge what we believed, what we saw and what we didn't understand? This will enable us to establish new and more convincing directions to walk on. Status quo demolishes curiosity. Curiosity opens up before us myriads of options, of better life and better relationships.

'Light Your Lantern' is a gift for the new-age professional. It uses the image of a lantern or a lamp with four wicks that can brighten the life of every reader. The reflections are woven together in the form of four wicks to design the reader into a brand-new person and help him to become a light in the world.

The first wick is titled: 'Come up Here'. It begins with the magic of self-confidence and exhorts everyone to live a life of beauty and positivity by building self-esteem, attitude and personality. This is the path to a higher realm of life. It lights up our own lanterns and gives light for the road ahead. It invites everyone to cherish the beauty of life.

I might have a lit lantern, but to walk ahead without stumbling, I need specific skills. The second wick elaborates on the skills required in our pursuit to light the lanterns of others. Here we make a poignant commitment to the prosperity of the universe. Here we test our readiness to learn, unlearn and relearn and to re-skill, up-skill and multi-skill. We identify skills to transform our talents into strengths and eliminate procrastination to go far together. In short, we focus on the critical skills required for today and tomorrow.

"It is better to light a candle than to curse the darkness", says an Irish blessing. The third wick inspires the reader to give his best in everything he does. This makes one immortal. One becomes noble by performing one's roles with commitment, ownership and passion. Those with light take risks to walk in darkness.

The final wick of 'Light Your Lantern' dwells on the riches of life. It gives oil for the wick to keep the flame alive. Darkness is a pain that can drive us or drown us. Light leads us to the future while living well in the present. The reader is invited to light the lamp within. "Nothing can dim the light that shines from within", says Maya Angelou.

"A lamp can have up to six wicks and each represents a different invocation," says Venkat, my friend, who is also a temple priest. 'Light Your Lantern' has four wicks. Four wicks represent all-around prosperity and abundance.

May 'Light Your Lantern' give you prosperity and progress in your life!

The Sacrifice of Light

The fusion inside the sun gives light and energy. This fusion of atoms creates a new element called the photon, the particle of light. They travel inside the sun for 40,000 years to reach its surface and then another 93 million miles at a speed of 300,000 km/second to reach the earth to illuminate it.

Isn't it an enduring sacrifice? Light gains nothing from this process. It only gives.

In the same way, when we experience the pressures and fusions of life, what we emanate should be light and life not darkness and death. Our life, words and deeds should illuminate light. It should light the lanterns of others not blow them off. "You are the light of the world", says Jesus Christ. The light in us is for the world.

I have met many ordinary men and women who became the light for others and helped them light their lanterns. Reggie Joseph is one such person who helped hundreds of young people to light their lanterns and become successful in life. He is a well-known educationist and a dedicated social worker in Silchar, known as the 'island of peace' in the Barak Valley of Assam.

About 20 years ago, he invited me to the village where he had a small technical school under a thatched roof to facilitate a two-month leadership program for University students. He had left his family in Kerala years ago to work in Assam. Being the youngest son of a planter, he could have lived a life of luxury. But he decided to light the lanterns of the downtrodden, the poor, the underprivileged, the discriminated and the weak. He became their light!

During the morning walks, he would take me around the villages. As we strolled by he would narrate his vision for the people. He would speak of making the place a centre for learning and research. He would even show me how and where the campus would be. He had a vivid picture of the future.

Though I scoffed at his dreams, he was determined. Years later, the miracle happened! There stands today a 60 acre campus with 80 class rooms, an eco-friendly park, a callisthenic park and an auditorium that can accommodate more than 1500 people. The Don Bosco school that he passionately developed stands as a testimony to his commitment to spread the light of knowledge, wisdom and goodness.

He is one of the most prominent educationists in Silchar today. As an influencer he has lit the lanterns of thousands of students who have become bureaucrats, politicians, public servants and educationists to build the nation. Instead of cursing the darkness, many like him decided to light candles.

With immense gratitude, I humbly dedicate 'Light Your Lantern' to them!

Light or Darkness?

Life is full of choices, both tough and easy. Choices multiply as science and technology progress. In 1980's I walked five miles to school. I had two choices: walk to school or stay at home. I chose to walk. In the next 40 years, more schools mushroomed and more options dawned for the youth of my village.

However, some choices remained constant irrespective of the changes that impacted history. It's the freedom to choose between light and darkness, between virtue and vice, between good and bad, to think positive and negative, to become ordinary or extraordinary. We choose to be compassionate, considerate, confident and courageous. We choose to become good! We choose to become light!

Once we choose light over darkness, it invades every sphere of our existence. We will never ever live in darkness! Light causes our egos to tumble down; with light we will thrive in any situation; we will emerge empowered after every crisis; diffuse the ballistic missiles of envy, greed and hatred aimed at us; we live happy and peaceful.

But it depends on the choices we make. "Human beings must make difficult choices. We are no longer in Eden. The world does not flow with milk and honey", says Todd G Buchholz, in his book 'New Ideas from Dead Economists'. Light helps us to make the right choices in life, to live in the light.

Right choices help us bring love, peace, forgiveness and compassion to a world that is in darkness. Slack, small, stale, static and sick minds terrorise and enslave progress and possibilities. Light liberates. It drives personal and professional transformation. It makes one resourceful and resilient, adept and adaptive, visionary and valuable, excellent and effective, compassionate and collaborative, humble and humane.

The Tiny Efforts of a Tiny Firefly

Rayarome, my little hamlet in Kerala, is protected on one side by mountains that are luxuriously vested in green while on the other side flows a river that sings beautiful melodies though at times during the monsoon, her dirge becomes ferocious and deadly. As children, we would spend hours in rainy nights watching the dance of the fireflies that appear in the twilight.

Those days we didn't have electricity or the fun of social media. The rich would listen to the music from radio while the poor would listen to the music of nature. We would lie on bed staring into the darkness and counting the innumerable fireflies: hundreds, thousands; and beyond as they twinkled in the sky. They nurtured our curiosity and imagination.

Every culture has formulated enough superstitions, folklores and romantic songs in galore about the firefly. My grandmother would tell that the fireflies were angels sent to give light to the villagers returning late from the fields after a day's heavy work. The Japanese believed that they were the souls of their ancestors. The Greeks believed that they were the messengers of goddess Diana. The Europeans believed that a firefly entering a house could cause an imminent death in the family.

However, science tells us that they emit rays to attract the perfect mate. The life span of a firefly is a few weeks and it dies sharing its light. The flames are the flames of selfless love!

They fly around remitting the ray of light, the ray of love and the ray of hope. They tell us about the dawn of a new season of hope. The tiny beetle emits a little glow to dispel the darkness a bit. It makes a little effort to spread love, to spread light.

'Light Your Lantern' is my humble and tiny endeavour to light up hearts. Everyone is a light for the world. Shall we then put our efforts together to make this world brighter?

Light Your Lantern! Or rather, be the Light. Let it shine!

Joshy Thomas

Come Up Here!

"I had another vision and saw an open door in heaven.

A voice that sounded like a trumpet said, 'Come up Here',

and I will show you what must happen after this."

The Book of Revelation

1 The Magic of Self-Confidence

Life is beautiful for those who live with confidence! They live with a noble purpose and confidence gives them the excitement to achieve this purpose. We too live exciting lives because we are achievers in one way or other. Confidence pushes us up to a higher realm of existence. It lights up our lanterns and inspires us to light the lanterns of others.

All achievers have one thing in common: self-confidence. It gives the courage to take greater risks and achieve more than we ever thought was possible.

This confidence gives a positive and realistic view of ourselves. It tells us to trust in our abilities and inspires us to believe we can achieve our dreams. It gives us the power to push ourselves beyond the horizon and perform miracles to surprise ourselves and the world around us. It gives magical results!

> External conditions or successes cannot give us confidence permanently because these conditions keep changing and our ambitions keep evolving.

Is there anyone in this world who wants to live unhappy? No. Everyone wants happiness. We go to the best school or college to get the best education; look for the best job with the highest compensation; look for the best spouse, the best house and the best of everything to become happy.

Though we have everything, yet we aren't happy. "What has gone wrong?" we ask ourselves. The mistake we commit is to look for happiness outside us. We imagine that if we succeed in our goals, we will become happy and as a result will become confident.

There are many role models and heroes who accomplished the impossible and possessed everything in the highest possible degree. However they failed to live with confidence and contentment. They lived a life of poverty because they lacked self-confidence. We too realize that external conditions or successes cannot give us confidence permanently because these conditions keep changing and our ambitions keep evolving.

"How can you be so happy always?" I asked Jose who was my senior in college. He was always joyful and we wondered what made him happy all the time. "I am happy even though things don't go as per my plan. I am happy even though things are not always right in my life. I am happy because I do not link my happiness with the happenings," he answered. He showed the true spirit of self-confidence!

How do We Know that We are Self-Confident?

Self-confident people have realistic expectations of themselves and others. Even if these expectations are not met they continue to remain positive, foster affectionate relationships, accept themselves as they are and look optimistically to conquer greater heights next time.

The self-confident feel good about themselves even when others don't appreciate or acknowledge their efforts. They hunger for their improvements and don't hunger for the approval of others. They are willing to risk their reputation and do what others are scared of doing because they believe in their ability to win. Jack Welch, the CEO of General Electricals, says, "Self-confidence gives us the courage and extends our reach. It lets us to take greater risks and achieve far more than we ever thought possible."

Have you noticed that when you are confident and courageous, the people around you also become the same? Just as courage is contagious, self-confidence too is  contagious. Confident people instil confidence in others.

In my previous book, 'Salt and Light: A Leader on a Pilgrimage', I dealt extensively with this contagious nature of courage and confidence. When you take risks others follow suit. When you leave the familiar shores and walk the extra mile, the others do the same.

Our self-confidence is expressed in our behaviour, body language, the way we dress, talk, look, walk etc.

What we say and think, how we act and relate and how we carry ourselves proclaim to the world whether we are confident or not.

When we experience a feeling of guilt, scepticism, self-shame, pride, fear, laziness, unforgiving attitude, depression, pretension, lack of trust in self and others, pessimism, inferiority complex, procrastination, self-doubt, submissiveness, isolation and jealousy, we are deteriorating in our confidence.

A self-confident person fears nothing, has attained the truth and is free of fear. He has won the battle over his inner life.

Be glad. There are ways by which one can build up self-confidence.

"When there is no enemy within, the enemies outside can do you no harm."
African Proverb

1. Have Faith in Yourself

Our self-confidence increases when we believe in our abilities to perform things and manage ourselves better in a given situation. All of us have innumerable talents and potential. The irony is that we are often not aware of them. To believe in our capabilities, we first of all, must identify what we have. For this we should do a SWOT analysis and realistically look at ourselves. It helps us to look at our strengths, weaknesses, opportunities and threats (SWOT) so as to discover our immense possibilities and potential.

Faith in our abilities boosts our self-confidence. We must dwell more on our strengths and use them to navigate through the challenges to minimize the weaknesses. Lack of self-confidence is the biggest enemy of life. "When there is no enemy within, the enemies outside can do you no harm," says an African proverb. We need to believe in ourselves. When we do this, our life becomes beautiful!

Abraham Lincoln is one of the most famous personalities in human history. He was emotionally mature, balanced in thinking, deprived of vices and lived a life of unimpeachable integrity with an abundance mindset. He taught us with his life that there is hope for everyone. He lived a life of confidence with complete faith in himself despite the colossal tragedies he faced in life.

He lost his mother when he was just nine; he lost his brother, sister and even his fiancé. He grew up under a cruel and harsh father who would beat him and severely punish him for anything and everything. He had a terrible marriage and two of his children died. He tasted failures in his career, lived in poverty, experienced depression and faced defeats in life. However he never gave up faith in himself and went on to become a role model of self-confidence.

Ruth Beitia Vila, the high jumper who won gold in the 2016 Rio Olympics, is another role model to emulate. She possessed immense faith in herself and would never give up on her dreams. Her life tells us that if we believe in ourselves and persist a little longer, the sweeter our life will become.

While participating in the 2004 Athens Olympics, she dreamt of gold only to reach 16th place among the contestants. However she didn't break down or give up. She continued to believe in herself and practised harder and longer. At the Beijing Olympics of 2008, she came 4th. Again in the 2012 London Olympics, she was the 4th in the competition.

Finally, after 12 years of persistence and self-confidence she struck gold during the Rio Olympics. What an amazing victory of faith, determination, perseverance and confidence!

2. Cherish Your Achievements

Have you ever thought about all those things that you can do successfully? We have an ocean of possibilities. We too are achievers. But we often brood over our failures to make our lives wretched. We forget about the small accomplishments and await the big ones that rarely appear on our way.

We need to think often of our successes if we wish to boost our self-confidence. The fear of failure prevents us from taking up anything new and challenging. Remember that we have so many good qualities and abilities and that we too can be successful if we perform our roles with our mind and heart.

Self-confidence boosts self-esteem, self-respect and self-image. If we focus on the achievements of the past, it will fill us with confidence to take risks and achieve success in future. "The only limit to the height of your achievement is yourself. Once you become daring and fearless, your life becomes limitless", says Dr. John Parankimalil, author and renowned educationist in North East India.

Self-confidence is learnable and is formed by conscious and repeated practice. Try to prepare a to-do list for each day and give your best to accomplish some of those activities. A simple way to gain confidence is to repeat these small achievements and celebrate them. Whenever we accomplish something we must celebrate it. Fill the mind with positive events that we can cherish instead of filling it with harmful, adverse and unforgettable incidents. When we celebrate we feel good about ourselves. This boosts our confidence.

3. Learn from Failures

"Failures are the best teachers." Everyone says so. But in real life, we are ashamed of failing. Our role models are those who accomplished much in life. They rarely tell us anything about their failures. Of course, we should learn from the successful. But the learning given by them is limited.

As a HRDian, I would invite people who had reached the zenith of fame to share the secret of their successes. However, most of them were unable to articulate and identify the things that made them succeed. Then we thought of inviting entrepreneurs who failed in their businesses. We realized that we could learn more from these people because they knew what

> Failures can ignite in us strength, confidence and resilience.

made them fail. When they narrated their stories of failure, sparks of innovation and inspiration ignited the minds of the listeners.

Can we look at our hurdles as springboards to bounce back? If we do so, we lay the foundations of a strong and confident nature. Failures have the power to ignite in us strength, confidence and resilience.

Stephen Edwin King, the author of many horror fictions and fantasy novels, had a horrifying start as a new author. He tasted many bitter failures in life before he reached stardom. His book was rejected by publishers 30 times! They repeatedly rubbished his idea of a horror fiction. Finally he even gave up his desire to become a writer.

One day his wife, Tabitha King, found the manuscript in a bin. He had not only thrown his script away, but also his dreams into the bin. However, his wife believed in his calibre and gave him confidence. He retrieved the manuscript and restarted to work on it. 'Carrie', the book rejected by him and his publishers, became a legend and Stephen Edwin King went on to become the 'King of Horror.'

Failures can teach us more than successes. "Doubts kill more dreams than failures ever will," says Suzy Kassem, philosopher and author of 'Rise Up and Salute the Sun.' Failure stories can give more inspiration than success stories.

'Fuckup Nights' is a global movement that acts as a platform for people who failed in business to share their experiences with a view to help others. These motivational talks inspire others to overcome the setbacks they have experienced in life and bounce back with vigour to take on the challenges.

4. Feel Good About Yourself

"No one can make us feel inferior without our permission," says Eleanor Roosevelt, the wife of US President Franklin D. Roosevelt. Though born into a wealthy and prominent family, she went through an unhappy childhood. She lost her parents when she was young. She had struggles with her mother-in-law and also faced marital problems with her husband.

> The secret of successful and happy living is to love oneself.

In order to remain positive and feel good about herself, she decided to pursue her calling by becoming a public personality. She became a prolific writer, activist, politician and even disagreed with her husband on many of his policies. However when President Roosevelt got infected with a paralytic illness, she motivated him to continue in politics.

All the setbacks she suffered didn't make her move away from what she believed. She kept pushing ahead because she felt good about herself. Her self-confidence brought her many achievements in life and thus became the most respected woman in the world.

How do we feel about ourselves? The secret of successful and happy living is to love oneself. When we are unhappy with ourselves we see unhappiness everywhere and as a result we make others unhappy. We must accept ourselves and feel good about the way we are. Our colour, size and shape do not matter. We must believe that the world can't be the same if we are not there.

Enjoy yourself once in a while by joining your friends for a night out; enjoy a good meal; go for a movie; play your favourite sports; take a few days off from work; spend time with your family and parents. Indulge in what you love. Live a few days for yourself.

Don't get worn out working hard to secure the future of your children. They are not dumb heads. They are talented and know how to take care of themselves. Laugh and forget yourself, enjoy some moments and run away from your work, stress and routine. This will make you feel good about yourself and will boost your confidence.

We need to treat ourselves with kindness. Forgive yourself when you have done something wrong instead of punishing yourself. Self-compassion and self-love are important to navigate the negative emotions that we experience. We cannot be compassionate to others if we are not compassionate to ourselves. Likewise, we cannot love others if we don't love ourselves first. Love yourself first if you want to love others.

5. Say No to Comparisons

Comparison and competition are the measures people use to value us. We are brought up by comparing. When

I scored less than my friend in school, my teachers and parents asked me why I scored less. Today when I get my increments, I compare them with my colleagues. When I see myself in a group photo, I compare my appearance with others.

Jealousy and envy are the fruits of comparison. We ruin our peace by comparing and competing with others. Competition makes us arrogant, envious and cunning. Comparison and competition diminish our confidence.

"Confidence is when you believe in yourself and your abilities. Arrogance is when you think you are better than others and act accordingly," says, Stewart Stafford, a popular author. As a result we have low self-esteem.

> Life is not a competition; neither is it a comparison. Each one is unique and there is no another version.

If you compare at all, compare to improve yourself. This is a healthy sign. Life is not a competition; neither is it a comparison. Each one is unique and there is no another version. So how can we compare one with another?

There was a happy crow that lived in a small city on the outskirts of a forest. He was content with himself and possessed good self-esteem. While on a hunting trip, one day, he saw a swan that looked more attractive than him.

"I am black and ugly while this swan is white and handsome", he said as he compared himself with the swan. "Swan might be the happiest bird in the world", he thought. This thought lowered his self-esteem. So he went to the swan and told him how he felt.

"I thought I was the happiest bird in the world till I saw a parrot", replied the swan. "The parrot has many colours and looks so charming. So he must be the happiest", said the swan as he flew off.

The crow, with a heavy heart, went to the parrot. "I lived a happy life until I saw a peacock. He is so colourful and must be the happiest", said the parrot.

The crow went in search of the peacock. After much effort, he found him caged in a zoo. The crow told him, "You are lucky and happy that you are handsome and colourful. So many people come to see you daily. I am ugly, black and no one even looks at me."

"You may think that I am the most handsome and the happiest. But because of my beauty, I am enslaved in this zoo and have no freedom to fly like you. I want to be a crow. I think you are the happiest bird because you have the freedom to go anywhere you please", lamented the peacock.

We compare, complain and remain unhappy. We don't value what we have. "Don't compare your life to others. There is no comparison between the sun and the moon. They shine when it's their time", says APJ Abdul Kalam. Can we look at what we have instead of comparing what we don't have with others?

6. Commit to Challenging Goals

Instead of comparing and competing, can we commit ourselves to challenging goals? This is a sure way to build one's confidence.

Goals can inspire confidence and can perform miracles in our lives. Greater the goals greater is our self-confidence. We should have both small goals and big goals. The achievement of small goals will give us enough enthusiasm and confidence to run towards bigger and more challenging goals.

We must think positively about our abilities to achieve our goals and reward ourselves when we achieve them. "If you hear a voice within you say, 'you cannot paint,' then by all means paint, and that voice will be silenced," says Vincent Van Gogh who was considered a failure and was misunderstood in his lifetime.

He lived a life of utter poverty and experienced immense depression in life. But he didn't give up. He painted around 2100 works which became the most treasured pieces of art in the world today. However, he and his works received fame only after his death. Self-confidence boosts itself when we take up challenging goals. It can make us immortal!

Our self-confidence depends on the degree of our commitment to a cause. If we are mediocre and half-hearted, the result will also be the same. We must commit ourselves to success and become passionate about what we do. Our commitment is expressed in our eagerness and desire to learn and develop new skills, knowledge and experience. Knowledge, skill and experience will give us the confidence to commit to a challenging goal.

7. Become Altruistic

Altruism is one of the best tools to gain confidence. Real confidence comes from doing good for others. When we are humble, compassionate, kind, empathetic and help others, we get a sense of satisfaction which leads us to believe in ourselves. External self-confidence may be achieved through deceit or competing against others. But real self-confidence comes only by loving others.

This is the confidence that Mother Teresa possessed. When people plotted against her work, she didn't lose hope

> "How far that little candle throws his beams! So shines a good deed in a weary world."
>
> William Shakespeare

because she had the confidence that help would come her way. She knew her little acts of kindness could create ripple effects across the world.

Prof. P.J. Joseph, my English professor and rector, at Salesian Training Institute, Shillong, would repeatedly remind us about the importance of altruism in life. "How far that little candle throws his beams! So shines a good deed in a weary world", he would quote William Shakespeare from 'The Merchant of Venice' to instill this value in us. "The more we live for others, the higher is our self-confidence," he says.

Benefits of Self-Confidence

"The most beautiful dress you can wear is your self-confidence," says Blake Lively, a Hollywood actress. So please put on your best dress of confidence because it gives you immense benefits. It leads to higher performance, healthy relationships and faster realization of possibilities. It gives one the willingness to take risks, ability to cope with challenging situations and provides higher resilience to bounce back when faced with obstacles. It makes one happy and peaceful. As a result, one begins to live a beautiful life!

An elephant and a mynah were great friends. But the elephant always felt sad because he could not fly like his friend. So one day he asked the mynah to teach him how to fly. The mynah agreed and led him to a cliff.

Pulling out a feather the mynah said: "Hold this feather tight in your mouth, flap your ears, jump down from this cliff and you will fly."

The elephant believed her words, held the feather tight in his mouth, flapped his ears and behold he began to fly!

He flew over the villages, the rivers and cities. People beneath applauded the elephant as he flew over them.

"What an amazing talent", they exclaimed. When he returned he told his friend, "Your feather is very powerful. Can I keep this feather with me because I want to use it whenever I want to fly?"

The mynah said, "It's not my feather. It's a hair from your tail. You only need to believe in your ability to fly. Believe in yourself and you will do miracles."

You can design your life beautiful! It can be dreadful if you don't believe in yourself.

Put on your dress of confidence to go up in life. Stretch your wings and unleash your limitless power. Your self-confidence will definitely help you to fly high in the sky. What a beautiful flight it will be!

2 Personality Powers Performance

Personality and performance are closely related. Wrong type of personality, especially at the leadership levels, can derail an organization and damage its brand. It can cause undesirable tension in organizations, societies and in families. It is the root cause of low morale, strikes and unrest and has ruined many mighty organizations. It has caused a lot of heartburns in relationships and has led to separations, turnovers and dissatisfactions.

Our personality can power us or can make us powerless. It depends on what type of personality we possess.

Though job-hopping is part of the modern lifestyle, organizations continue to invest in people to retain them. Retention is a challenge. I believe the biggest challenge, however, is to hire and treasure the best personalities.

Our personalities drive our behaviours and colour our work. A person who is diligent, disciplined, meticulous and passionate will produce a hundredfold and will be more productive than the one who is careless, lethargic, critical and undisciplined. While on the one hand, an extroverted leader who is full of zeal, energy and excitement can influence his team much better than a pessimistic introvert, on the other hand, an innovative, humble, silent and optimistic introvert can touch the hearts of his team and customers much deeper with his creative solutions and products than a noisy extrovert.

Organizations invest huge to assess the personality styles of their employees using various assessment tools with a view to help them to become more productive. Often it remains an investment that brings no return. These massive reports generated by expensive assessments are stored in archives and seldom used to improve behaviour or personalities.

Gig work culture is the talk of the town today. The 'future of work' that experts talk of is present here and now. The life of full-time employment is reaching its grave! Freelancers and part-timers will take over full-timers soon. Moonlighting is loved and hated at the same time.

Organizations look for employees who will work hard, innovate and contribute to their growth. They hunt for digital savvy and futurist talents. Are we bypassing the best with the right personalities in this process? What should we do to improve our personalities and become the right fit?

The best way to power performance is to power personalities.

What is Personality?

Personality is the study of the unique traits of an individual. The word 'personality' comes from the Latin word 'persona' which means 'mask'. Thus personality came to be associated with a person's outward appearance. People could mask and succeed too!

But today, we know that personality doesn't mean external appearances alone. It is rather a dynamically organized totality of personal traits which distinguish one individual from another. It is the total picture of a person, consisting of his inner and outer being. It encompasses his feelings, thoughts and behaviours.

It is said that the greatest building in the world is 'building personalities.' However our schools and colleges taught us very little as to how to build our personalities. We learnt Mathematics, Science, History, Robotics, Data Analytics and Aero Dynamics; but nothing about ourselves. In our mad rush for success and fame, we seldom pause to discover who we are.

Traditionally, experts opine that personality consists of the four dimensions of a person: physical, social, mental and spiritual. Today's highly digitalized world pushes us to add a fifth dimension called the digital dimension. If we want to develop our personality, we need to build these five areas of our life. We must develop and integrate these five aspects of our personality to lead a life of fullness. And that will power our performance.

1. Physical Dimension

The physical dimension plays an important role in the development of one's personality. A good and healthy physique can enhance one's personality and self-esteem. It includes our health, strength and withstanding capacity and not merely our physical structure, colour or features.

It also tells how we present ourselves to others: our dress code, lifestyle, behaviours, grooming and etiquette. All these matter. The better dressed we are, the more sure we are to attract people to us.

People have become conscious of their physique. They frequent gyms and exercise regularly to keep themselves fit and healthy.

We communicate our personality by the way we walk, stand, sit, talk, look and act. All that we do communicate the level of our personality. Thus learning to keep oneself fit and healthy and to present oneself in a decent and socially acceptable manner is an art that a person needs to learn in order to develop a better personality.

Grooming is part of the corporate training curriculum in many organizations. In my leadership sessions, I use the concept of 'LAW of Personality' to help the leaders. 'L' stands for 'look.' It refers to the importance of demonstrating the best impression right at the first second of meeting another person.

'A' stands for 'actions.' We need to take care of our posture, movements, appearance and actions.

'W' stands for the words we use. Do we articulately communicate our ideas and use our words politely to build relationships? Do we indulge in loose talk to gain popularity or do we talk assertively to gain respect?

If we look around, we can find many leaders who have become successful because they abide by this LAW of Personality.

Appearances can deceive us. Having an attractive physical feature is no guarantee for a respectable personality. Mary Ann Bevan, who won the 'Ugliest Woman Contest' in 1914, was actually beautiful internally. She was born in London in a family of eight children. She had an excellent job as a nurse and was happily married with four children when a tragedy struck her.

She was infected with acromegaly which caused distortion in body and abnormal growth in facial features. After the death of her husband, she became the only breadwinner for the family. However she had to leave her job soon because of her illness.

> "Beauty is not in the face; it's a light in the heart."
>
> Kahlil Gibran

In order to take care of her family, she decided to participate in the most humiliating contest called the 'Ugliest Woman Contest.' The money that she got by winning the contest was not sufficient to take care of the family. So she joined a circus company as a joker where people would make fun of her appearance and would ridicule her. But she went through these because she was committed to a cause. She experienced humiliation so that her children could have a better quality of life.

She passed away in 1933 leaving us a legacy that real beauty lies hidden within the physical appearances we carry. She was in fact one of the most beautiful women in the world! "Beauty is not in the face; it's a light in the heart", says Kahlil Gibran, writer and philosopher.

2. Social Dimension

It refers to our ability to relate to others. Human beings are social beings. We can't live as islands. We need to connect, communicate and collaborate with others if we want to improve our performance and become better humans. We need to learn the art of creating lasting and effective relationships in today's world of 'use and throw away' culture. We need to learn the art of staying connected to others, if we wish to power our performance.

We love to globalize indifference. We have become selfish and greedy to the core that we don't feel the pain of even our dear ones. It's high time we re-planted in ourselves the seeds of social values like equity, equality, justice, fairness and compassion.

A person, who loves and cares for others without bias and assumptions, has a more pleasing personality. Contributing to society and taking care of others is our responsibility. We will never be forgotten for our humanitarian and selfless services.

"I don't know what your destiny will be, but one thing I do know: the ones among you who will be really great are those who serve," says Albert Schweitzer, theologian, author and the recipient of Nobel Prize in 1952. People who serve receive much respect and love. In fact we are called to serve.

> "Whoever wants to be great among you must be your servant."
>
> **Jesus Christ**

"Whoever wants to be great among you must be your servant", says Jesus Christ. He not only preached this but showed it in action. During the Last Supper, he washed the feet of his disciples, an act that was performed by servants. He exhibited greatness in action.

If we dislike others, they too will dislike us. Construct good relationships with those around and they will stand by us when we least expect. We need to become more an extrovert who is sociable, constructive, assertive and supportive. Give joy to everyone; smile always and more so when things go wrong. Have a 'hi' or a 'hello' for everyone we meet. Invest in building networks. Make sure to meet a new person a day. Enhance the circle of friends and well-wishers. These may appear prescriptive but are proven medicines to strengthen one's social dimension.

3. Mental Dimension

Mental dimension refers to our intellectual capacity. A person who is intuitive, intelligent, clever and creative is always respected and sought after. He is admired for his discoveries, innovations and excellent thoughts. He uses his common sense, brain and imagination to become more creative.

People admire his intelligence and smartness. He takes risks and challenges and is willing to walk the un-trodden paths. He learns daily to broaden the horizons of his knowledge. He is a walking encyclopedia in his area of expertise. He readily helps his colleagues when they are clueless and gives convincing solutions when they seek guidance. He consistently demonstrates expertise. We respect his intelligence and thinking.

The world is fortunate to have many such people who are intelligent and at the same time humble and positive. They think positive about themselves and others. They treat everyone with utmost respect and esteem. They  see something good in everybody, in everything and this creates a positive atmosphere around. People love their company and admire their personality.

Dr. APJ Abdul Kalam stands out as a person of immense intelligence, deep humility and selfless love for the youth. His life was rooted in values and principles.

From being the son of a boatman from a remote village in Tamil Nadu, he went on to become the President of India. He was an aerospace scientist, was the missile man of India, was the President and was an outstanding academician but more than all he was a humble soul who loved the youth.

He spent most of his energy and time to nurture the dreams of youth and helped them to build their future. His love for students drove him to share his knowledge across the country till the moment of his death on 27 July 2015 while delivering a lecture to a group of students at IIM Shillong. He will forever remain a role model because of his immense knowledge, humility, dedication to youth, strength of character and amiable personality.

Like Dr. Kalam, we all have the resources and capabilities to succeed. Our body and brain are similar to the best scientists, artists or athletes. We all have millions of neurons and each is more powerful than the most powerful computer. We are as powerful and capable as anybody else on this planet.

We blame God, society, education and environment. We accuse them as biased. We wonder why some are more privileged, talented or capable. We focus on our deprivation. We are so because we are like those who own the most luxurious car in the world but don't know how to drive. We keep the car in the garage. Cars are for the road not for the garage. Similarly, we store our resources and keep them idle.

4. Digital Dimension

My book on leadership, 'The Salt and Light: A Leader on a Pilgrimage', discusses extensively on the digital dimension of a person. We live in a digital era. Digitalization has become an extension of ourselves. We are no more merely physical, social, intellectual or even spiritual selves. We have an element of digitalness in us. The digital workplace of today demands digital qualities from us.

The world in recent years has witnessed massive transformations and disruptions caused by the digital revolution. What we know today becomes outdated the next day. To live fully, we have to become digital literate and should be conversant with digital technology and social media.

Concepts like Artificial Intelligence, Big Data Analytics, Internet of Things, Machine Learning, Deep Learning, Augmented and Virtual Realities, Business Intelligence etc. are sweeping across all areas of our lives. People are investing massively to equip themselves with digital mindsets to steer themselves through the waves of sudden, unpredicted and unprecedented changes that are mounting on them often by surprise.

The digital world of today has unfolded before us innumerable opportunities to speed up our operations and thus make a lasting impression. These disruptions force us to make significant changes in our mindset. When we reinforce our traditional ways of working with cutting-edge digital technology, supported by digital tools we leverage the manifold opportunities that unfold before us.

People with a digital dimension are fast and furious to apply different technologies like Cloud, Analytics, Data Management, Blockchain etc. to help them in their forecasting and decision-making processes. They definitely will outperform the digitally illiterate in the coming days. They possess the acumen to appreciate and understand the digital transformation taking place in the world. The digital dimension gives massive power to boost one's performance. The winners are those who adopt, integrate and use technology in everything they do.

However we are also victims and slaves of this digital onslaught. Till recently we trainers were busy facilitating programs on 'Work-Life Balance'. Today there is nothing called work-life balance. It's work-digital-life balance. We spend some time at work. We spend some time at home too.

We are enslaved to social media. Have you ever estimated the amount of screen time you spend on gadgets? Shall we take up a challenge to spend a day without mobiles?

5. Spiritual Dimension

It refers to how we uphold values and principles of life and how we relate with the divine. It is the inner power that guides our conscience and behaviour. It expresses itself in our moral values and in our sense of duty, responsibility and accountability. It gives us the power for self-confidence, leadership, initiatives, willpower and self-discipline.

It makes us authentic and genuine when we are alone and in the company of others. Our spiritual dimension gets reflected in our sincerity, honesty, truthfulness, kindness and gentleness. A deep union with the divine person and a selfless love for humanity can enhance our personality. This enables us to control our emotions and live by values and thus become a 'super hero'.

> Spiritual people display positive emotions like love, forgiveness, kindness, hope, loyalty, trust and optimism.

People will admire us if we make efforts to minimize our fear and anxiety, our hatred and anger, our jealousness and suspicion. Spiritual people display positive emotions like love, forgiveness, kindness, hope, loyalty, trust and optimism. For this to happen, we should live not by our feelings alone but by our values as well.

We need to have good personalities to attract, enthuse, influence, motivate and lead others and ourselves to reach the optimum level of performance. Success depends more on personality and very little on knowledge, skills and resources. It is said that a person with a magnanimous personality can brighten the room he enters. He can soothe, calm and thrill people. He can catalyze performance and positive spirits.

True greatness does not come from the wealth we possess, the car we drive or the house we live in. It does not matter how many zeroes are there in our salary or the titles we carry next to our name or the number of trophies displayed in our showcases. It does not come from the number of people we command or lead. It is not inherited nor is it part of our DNA.

"Greatness is the conquest of self and giving oneself out in service," says Dr. John Parankimalil author and renowned educator. The great soul responds to his  inner calling and lives by values; he is persistent in all that is right and good; generous with the weak and poor; sacrifices himself for the benefit of others; adds value to the world. He brings light!

One of the greatest geniuses India has given to the world is CV Raman. His commitment to scientific research gave our nation many laurels. He introduced the Raman Effect to the world which explained the phenomena of light dispersing itself as it travels through a prism. This deflection causes changes in its wavelength and amplitude. This discovery which was the fruit of his commitment paved the way for the invention of lasers.

He won the Nobel Prize for Physics in 1930 in addition to many other awards and recognitions from across the world.

He began to display his intellectual calibre and innovative thinking even as a young child. He was the second among 8 children. His father was a high school teacher earning a meagre salary. Difficulties didn't deter him from pursuing his goal. He would read all the books his father had and would walk to the library to collect more books.

At the age of 19, he became an Assistant Accountant General in Calcutta and in 1933, became the first Indian to hold the post of Director of the Indian Institute of Science in Bangalore.

He was firm in his convictions and believed in his strengths. When foreign Universities invited him to come to their countries to learn from them he asked them to come to India to learn from him. He was so confident that he would win the Nobel Prize that he booked his tickets to Sweden four months before the results were announced. This was the self-confidence he had. His personality powered his performance and confidence.

At the same time, he was deeply human and deeply humble. He believed that becoming a good person was more important than

> "Becoming a good person is more important than the worship we offer."
>
> CV Raman

the worship he offered. He also believed in presenting himself well in public. He was well groomed, polite and respected people irrespective of their background. When people asked him why he wore a turban which was not part of his traditional attire, he replied humbly, "Everyone is praising me so much that my ego is swelling up. My turban controls my ego."

CV Raman is a role model for us as we build up our personalities. It doesn't matter where we come from, what we believe in, what we have or who we are. What matters in life is what we do with what we have.

One of the ways by which we can enhance our performance, achieve our goals and reach happiness is by investing in our personality. We need to take care of the physical, social, mental, digital and spiritual areas of our life.

People are different; even those from the same family differ to a great extent. They differ not only in appearance but also in feelings, thoughts, aspirations, ideas and actions. The environment, education, upbringing and genetics condition us. Based on these we make our decisions.

"Environments in which we grew up affect our personalities and lifestyle choices for either good or bad", says Sreenidhi SK, author and founder, Oscar Murphy International.

In spite of all these conditionings we can choose to develop in us a pleasing, attractive and winning personality. We need to improve our personalities first to improve our performance. Our personality is the reflection of our inner values.

There are hospitals that can help us to correct our external appearances through plastic and dental surgeries. We live in an era that stresses so much on the external appearances of an individual.

Every city has seen a mushrooming of gyms and fitness centres. Every other person we meet is a yoga guru or an aerobic trainer. People are ready to invest any amount to alter the way they appear.

But the alteration required is deep within: the way we think, act, react and respond. This transformation should be based on our spiritual dimension.

We will bloom into winning personalities the moment we decide to focus more on the spiritual dimension of our personality. When we do that, our personalities will begin to power performance.

3 Self-Awareness: The Key to Unleash Your Potential

"Tell me who you are." My teacher would ask us repeatedly while we were in school. "Now please don't tell me your name or about your family history", she would warn us. "Can you tell me who you are?" She would insist. As kids, we never had any answer either.

Well, it's one of the toughest questions for anyone to answer.

"Knowing oneself is the beginning of all wisdom," says Aristotle, the Greek philosopher. We tend to fail in our ventures because we don't

> "Knowing oneself is the beginning of all wisdom."
> Aristotle

know who we are. We don't know what we want; we don't know where we are heading; we don't know what we are good at. We have plenty of knowledge about the external world but fail to understand who we are. We are experts when it comes to evaluating others but don't know how to evaluate ourselves.

Self-awareness is the biggest contributor to one's success and happiness. Happy people evaluate and improve themselves while the unhappy evaluate and judge others.

During a Faculty Development Program that I attended years ago, Prof. Sunney Tharappan, founder, College of Leadership and Human Resources Development, Mangalore, narrated the story of a musk deer. The deer wanders around the whole day, searching for the source of the musk scent. It goes to sleep in the evening unhappy because it is not successful in identifying the source of the musk. The foolish deer doesn't know that the musk emanates from its own body.

Similarly, we too, look for greatness outside us. We compare ourselves with others and conclude that we don't have talents like others. As a result, we fail to discover our immense potential.

We need to believe in ourselves to restore our self-respect, self-esteem and self-confidence. If we want to conquer an empire, first, we must conquer ourselves. Self-unawareness is the biggest obstacle to our success, not the lack of resources or opportunities.

How to Attain Self-Awareness?

Self-awareness is unattainable to most of us because we think it is some philosophical or metaphysical status which can be reached only by ascetics, hermits or sanyasis. It is simple not complex; it is reachable to ordinary people like us too. It is to know ourselves: who we really are and who we see ourselves to be. To do this, we need to move from unconscious incompetence to conscious incompetence.

Many people are unaware of their incompetence. Only when we become conscious of our incompetence, will we be able to move to the stage of conscious competence.

The ultimate stage we can reach is called the unconscious competence where competence becomes a part of our very being. It is based on our knowledge about ourselves. It is the self-actualization of oneself and is never based on the perceptions of others.

Stanford Research Institute in 1960 developed a self-awareness tool called the SWOT. It is the easiest way to self-awareness. An honest SWOT analysis reveals one's strengths, weaknesses, opportunities and threats.

Shall we do a SWOT? Try to write them down on a sheet of paper. Write also how you can use these strengths in concrete situations. I need to discover the qualities, strengths, abilities and capabilities that make me a unique person in this world. It is to know who we are deep inside.

It helps us become aware of how we behave in critical times. The way we behave in normal times is different from the way we behave in critical times. We need to become aware of both.

SWOT Analysis

Strength	Weakness
Opportunity	Threat

Shall we use our numerous strengths to create a propitious niche where we can excel? We are important in this world. When we value our worth as a person, acknowledge our gifts with joy and use them to the best of our ability, we reach excellence.

Think often as a person possessing immense qualities. We must appreciate ourselves when we accomplish something. Don't wait for others to appreciate us; they may never do or they may never think of it as necessary. We must tell ourselves that we are important, remarkable and unique.

Sometimes it's ok to boast about ourselves. Don't be too humble all the time. Tell people often what we are good at and show them that we are masters in that task. Think of the accomplishments and convince them that we can accomplish greater things.

We are what we think. So think positively. Our thoughts about ourselves very powerfully influence us in our actions. We must believe that we are people with immense potential, that we are the best human beings.

Another way to reach self-awareness is to seek the help of others. Participate in a Johari Window exercise, proposed by Joseph Luft and Harry Ingham. This is a powerful tool to understand ourselves and the way we relate to others. It tells us how receptive and sincere we are when we interact with others and seek their feedback. Here we list down our knowledge about ourselves and also seek the opinions of others.

We need to widen the quadrant of the 'open area' through self-disclosure and feedback. We need to make the blind and secret areas of our lives smaller and allow the open area to become larger. This happens when I let you know me and by knowing what you think of me. This helps me to grow in my self-awareness.

Johari Window

	Known to Self	Unknown to Self
Known to Others	Open	Blind
Unknown to Others	Hidden	Unknown

Steps to Reach Self-Awareness

Once we become aware of ourselves, we need to do three more things to become more effective. First, based on the SWOT analysis or Johari Window, we need to list down the areas that need our attention. These are areas where we need to improve. It may be our interpersonal skills, conflict management styles, decision making or collaborative skills that require our focus.

Once we know the areas of improvement, the next step is to prepare an action plan. Design a concrete action plan to work on the weaknesses. While preparing this plan, it is beneficial to fix a target and a standard that will help us to reach the required changes and assess ourselves against some of the best and most acceptable behaviors.

The third step is to act on our plans. Many people have lovely plans that remain on paper. We should take some baby steps to improve our weak areas. It is good to have some coaches and mentors who can guide and coach us at this stage.

What we truly are is often different from what we perceive of ourselves. We know so little about ourselves and as a result we have a poor self-image. We are more conscious of our limitations and shortcomings than our strengths and talents. Our wrong self-image conditions our thought about ourselves and others and thus we feel increasingly inferior and never discover who we are.

Self-awareness leads us to recognize our strengths and opportunities. This fills us with optimism and gives us the key to unleash our immense potential.

William Somerset Maugham was one of the highest paid novelists of his time. It was not luck that brought him success. Rather it was his willingness to replace his weakness with his strength and his desire to focus on opportunities. He was poor and orphaned. More than poverty, what affected him most was his stammering. These insecurities forced him to withdraw from social events.

He was a qualified medical practitioner but decided to become a writer. This was his strength. As a successful writer, he still stammered. "What has influenced my life more than anything else has been my stammer. If I didn't have this, I would have become a don", he would say of his weakness. His adversity became his ally.

Benefits of Self-Awareness

Having known who we are, the next thing to do is to live according to this awareness. This means to live according to our true nature. Don't pretend to be someone else. If we live an unauthentic life, we are going to be lunatics  soon due to the stress and strain we create by acting out someone else's life. On the other hand, when we live an authentic life we genuinely become happy and peaceful.

Self-awareness and performance are related. The moment we truly discover who we are, we will begin to live a more competent and happy life. It helps us to match ourselves with the world of work and enables us to choose the right career based on our skills, values, attitudes, aptitudes, interests, motivation and expectations.

Another result of self-awareness is high-quality relationships and fulfilling personal lives. When we understand ourselves, the herculean task of understanding others becomes easy. When we know our strengths, values, perceptions and personalities, we will appreciate the values, styles, strengths and personalities of others. This helps in building lasting and high-quality relationships.

Self-awareness helps us to develop good interpersonal skills. We make huge blunders by merely limiting our judgments about others based on our biased observations.

If we want to relate to others, we need to go out of our comfort zones, come out of the 'fences' surrounding our cubicles, meet and interact with people, learn from them and expand our horizons. When we converse with them we learn more, build a good rapport and grow up respectable.

People with high self-awareness grow in conviction and competence and are willing to accept responsibility. They face life with optimism and lead fulfilling lives. They are highly motivated, energetic, ambitious and performance oriented. They discover avenues to unleash their potential and realize their dreams. In short, they get what they want.

Instant Gratification Slows Self-Awareness

We all want things instantly. We live in a fast-moving culture with fast food, quick information, products and services at our fingertips. We rely more on social media friendships than real-life friends. We look for appreciation and affirmation from social media contacts and forget to appreciate people around us. We want things and results at the moment.

This desire for instant pleasure, instant happiness and instant gratification has made us disconnected, impatient and ineffective. This gives us short-term, immediate and small pleasure by sacrificing lasting happiness that might come later.

Sigmund Freud, the founder of psychoanalysis who suggested an innovative way to cure people with mental health problems through a dialogue between the doctor and his patient, called it the 'Pleasure Principle.' This drive to avoid pain and experience pleasure is inherently present in everyone.

Everyone is motivated by this pleasure principle. As a result, self-denial, mortification and delay of gratifications are thought to be in the realm of those who renounce the pleasures of this world. Sadly, people wrongly associate self-awareness with ascetic life.

Self-awareness is a patient activity. It cannot be attained instantly in two minutes. At the same time, it is not the privilege of ascetics or hermits. It is reachable to anyone who sincerely pursues it. We are the best assessor of ourselves if we do it honestly. As we said, self-evaluation is not only to discover our strengths but also to reveal our loopholes and make action plans to rectify them.

It is human nature to be liberal while we evaluate ourselves and unduly critical while we evaluate others. We indulge in gratification through destructive talk, overeating, by watching or engaging in immoral acts, involving in self-defeating habits or by living a sedentary lifestyle.

Self-gratification is the enemy of self-awareness. If we are serious to walk on the road to self-awareness, then we must learn to manage, control and rein our gratifying tendencies.

Rules for Doing a Self–Evaluation

As we said, to become aware of ourselves, we need to evaluate who we are. While doing this, we must remember the following rules.

First of all, we must be honest and sincere while

doing the evaluation. We are doing it because we want to enjoy its fruits. So we shouldn't fake it for the sake of pleasing others. It is for our development and growth.

Hunt for the most genuine feedback from others. For this, we must have the courage to accept the feedback without defence or attacking the giver. This is the second rule we must follow. If positive feedback motivates us, the negative will help us to become perfect.

The third rule is to accept the feedback without comparison. We need to resist our tendency to compare ourselves with others when some negative things are pointed out to us. The whole world might be doing it. But we are interested in our growth; so why should we worry about what the world is doing? We want to change ourselves and become better.

The next rule is to question our beliefs and values. When we become negative, lethargic, pessimistic or worried it's good to pause and ask, 'why are we so?' We will find answers that will help us to correct ourselves instead of blaming the world.

Finally, start the self-awareness journey by taking time off the busy schedule to discover ourselves and our immense potential.

Finding Strength in Weakness

One of my all-time favourite authors is Brian Cavanaugh. In his famous book, "Sower's Seeds", he narrates the inspiring story of Wilma Rudolph who won three Olympic Gold Medals.

She was born in a poor family in Tennessee as the 20th of 22 children. What more, she was born premature and her parents doubted her survival. "She wouldn't survive the winter," concluded the villagers.

At the age of four, an attack of pneumonia and scarlet fever left her paralyzed. She was given an iron leg brace so that she could walk the minimum.

Her mother, however, believed in her power and would encourage her to walk and live like any other child in the family. As a result she became very bright and talented.

"You can do whatever you want and you will achieve whatever you desire in life if you go for it," assured the mother.

"What you need is not a perfect physique but a strong faith in God, persistence in your desire, courage in taking risks and a never say die attitude", she reminded her daughter.

The doctors were pessimistic about a recovery. But to the surprise of the medical staff, one day at the age of nine, she removed her leg brace and began to walk with faltering steps. She was determined. She didn't want to use a leg brace and wanted to live like the other children.

"I want to join the running race in school", she told her family once during dinner. Everyone laughed at it first and then objected to her idea except her mother. With her mother's support and encouragement, at the age of 13, she participated in the running race at school. As expected, she came last. But her indomitable spirit didn't give up. She joined every race in school and in every race, she was the last.

Her teachers asked her to quit. Her siblings begged her to give up her ambition. Her friends laughed at her determination. Her critics ridiculed her efforts. But she knew what her strength was. She knew she could succeed.

Then came the day on which during a race she was not the last. She came second last. She continued to race. One day, to everybody's surprise, she won the race. From then on every race that she participated she won!

"When the sun is shining I can do anything; no mountain is too high, no trouble is too difficult to overcome", she believed.

She went on to compete in the Olympics. In 100 meter race Wilma won. She won again in 200 meter race. Finally in 400 meter relay race too she won the gold. A fragile girl with weak health but with fierce determination and who knew her strength and talents won three gold medals. Wilma is a role model for everyone.

"Your weakness can make you vulnerable, but so can your strengths", says Michael D Watkins in his best seller 'The First 90 Days'. Doing what we did best yesterday may become our biggest source of incompetence. "To a person with a hammer, everything looks like a nail", says Abraham Maslow.

Is a strength forever a strength? Probably not.

Live Up to Your Potential

When we discover our strengths we become winners irrespective of who we are. It doesn't matter who we are and where we come from. What we do with what God has given us: this only matters in life. If we don't discover our strengths we will be like the musk deer searching for excellence elsewhere.

> What matters in life is your passion not your position!

A bird on a dry branch is not afraid of the storm. If the branch breaks, it has the capability to fly and search for another branch. Sit on your strength not on your positions. Sit comfortably without fear because you know what your strengths and opportunities are. As we said, what matters in life is our passion not our position!

We have won many races in life. From womb to tomb, we race to win. Our birth was not a coincident or an accident. It was a divine plan and God wanted us to win. "People are designed for accomplishments, engineered for success and endowed with seeds of greatness", says Zig Ziglar, the management guru.

Everyone has a unique role to play in this world. What each one of us can achieve no one else can!

What others do, I don't need to do. We are created for big things and hence we need to dream big and accomplish big. We are gifted with immense potential. The future belongs to those who are ready to unleash their potential.

Do we plan to unleash our potential or do we plan to hide it? The winners unleash it, defy the equilibrium, challenge the paradigm and chart new paths for others to follow.

Years ago, a group of villagers were renovating an ancient temple in their village. They discovered a mud statue which they kept aside as they continued to work. The work had to be called off soon due to heavy rain.

The next morning when they returned to resume the work, they were astonished to see a golden statue in the place of the mud statue. The people who built the temple years ago had covered the golden statue with mud to protect it from robbers.

The rain washed off the mud and now the statue was glowing in the morning sun. The villagers all these years were unaware of the preciousness of this statue. The rain revealed the invisible visible.

Psychologists say that humans possess three faculties: the ability to think, feel and behave. We have the capability to think, analyze and evaluate. We also have the ability to feel different emotions like happiness, sadness, anger and fear. We have the freedom to choose our behaviours like the way we react, say or do.

My self-image is the result of what I think about myself. My self-esteem is the outcome of what I feel about myself. It tells how I respect myself. The way I react or respond to situations and people defines my self-confidence. Self-awareness is a combination of all these three faculties of thinking, feeling and behaving.

Do we know about ourselves? We know everything about everybody! Except about us!

Vincent William van Gogh lived a life of deep depression. He was a failure and unsuccessful as a painter while alive. People attribute lack of self-awareness as the reason for such a life of misery, leading to his death at the age of 37.

It is said that he painted his own portrait more than 35 times! Why? Each time, he failed to understand himself and his complete identity. Each of these portraits was different. "It is not only difficult to know oneself, it is not easy to paint oneself either", he confined to his friends.

There is gold in each one of us. Divinity dwells in every heart. Unfortunately, we have covered it with hard shells of selfishness, greed, arrogance, anger and pride. If we allow these to be washed off, the gold will shine out.

We don't know who we are or what we possess. Lack of self-awareness sabotage our progress.

"We are so used to doing what we've always done that we don't stop to question whether it's the right thing to do at all. Many of our failures in performance are largely attributable to a lack of self-awareness", says James Clear in his celebrated book, Atomic Habits.

Understanding oneself is a tedious and painful process. Not as easy as we say. And those who discover themselves will surely radiate with glory.

As Buddha says, "Knowing others is wisdom. Knowing oneself is enlightenment." Become aware to become enlightened. Unleash your huge potential to make a mark!

4

Make a Mark with High Self-Esteem

Self-esteem is the way we feel and think about ourselves. It literally means 'having no uncertainties about one's abilities.' It is not inborn but is built up as a person grows up. It's the result of one's belief in one's worth and depends on how one thinks about oneself.

It makes us more self-confident, paves the way for effective relationships, helps us to pursue a challenging and thrilling career, takes us to our cherished goals and gives us the pride to accept ourselves as we are.

The successes in life depend to a large extent on one's self-esteem. Those with high self-esteem are more competent and effective in whatever they do. They suffer less from negative emotions and depression. They cope with life's problems and failures better and lead happy and contented lives. It affects everything that they do. When faced with challenging situations, people with high self-esteem make the right choices in life.

> Our perception of ourselves critically influences our performance, relationships and professional and personal life.

Our self-esteem is affected by the way we feel about ourselves: our physique, appearance, social status, family background, upbringing, education, wealth etc. All these factors contribute to the development of positive self-esteem. When we have low self-esteem we become sensitive to our weaknesses both internal and external. As a result, we withdraw ourselves to live lonely lives.

Our perception of ourselves critically influences our performance, relationships and professional and personal life. It is proved that people with high self-esteem are optimistic and happy. They build strong convictions, take responsibility and risks, make things happen, welcome challenges, accept changes and nurture relationships. They are self-motivated, receive criticism, walk the road less travelled, appreciate, admire and respect others honestly. In short, they live their lives with fulfilment.

It is easy to identify people who have low self-esteem. They are most of the time negative, jealous, sorrowful and indulge in gossip. They are fear creators and destroy the character and reputation of others through their unjust criticisms. They live with pessimism, sadism, pride, ego and arrogance. They love bullying others, are selfish, greedy and defensive. They blame others for their failures. They are biased, insincere and steal the appreciation of others.

The ultimate question is: 'to which group do we belong?' Are we people with high self-esteem? Remember, we are responsible for our self-esteem.

Here are some steps that can help us to develop our self-esteem.

1. Focus on Possibilities

We are full of possibilities, immense potential and innovative spirits. But where do we focus our attention to: on our potential, talents, abilities or on our limitations and failures?

We have enough possibilities and qualities to live a happy and fulfilled life. We need to discover who we are. When we think of our strengths, of things that we can do exceptionally well and of our many achievements our self-esteem shoots up.

Mark Joseph Inglis, the mountaineer from New Zealand reached the zenith of Mount Everest in May 2006 after 40 days of strenuous climb. Though many had already conquered Everest, the world celebrated the achievements of Mark because here was a man who reached the pinnacle of the tallest mountain in the world using his artificial legs.

In 1983 as a 23 year old, while climbing Mount Cook in New Zealand, he was frost-bitten and as a result both his legs had to be amputated. Though he lost his legs, he didn't lose his hope. Though he was amputated, his dreams remained intact. Though the world judged him as a failure he believed in his possibilities.

He learnt to walk using a pair of prosthetic legs and continued to invest in his self-esteem till he reached his goal and defeated Everest. He became the first amputated person to reach Everest.

> We are like an atom bomb ready to explode and energize this world.

Focusing on our possibilities will help us to gain new skills and new knowledge which in turn will give us more self-confidence. We have no limitations; so never impose limits on your dreams, on your potential, on your ability to learn and grow. We have so much power within us. We are like an atom bomb ready to explode and energize this world. We must allow our creative and innovative enthusiasm to flow beyond all limits and space.

If we learn continuously to expand the treasures of knowledge and invest sufficiently to upgrade our skills regularly, we will become star performers and reach the zenith with much ease.

2. Embarrass the Failure

Failures will always be there; at times in life they may defeat and embarrass us. With our self-esteem it is possible to transform these limitations and failures into opportunities for growth and development.

We are an ocean of possibilities and not a bundle of failures. When we forget the failures, we will surprise ourselves. We are like an elephant with colossal exuberance that is chained to an imaginary and fragile pole. We need to discover that we have the power to unchain ourselves and that we can live free.

We must measure success and failures with optimism and learn from failures instead of blaming the world. Every failure is a stepping-stone towards success. So we have no reason to be worried even when we fail.

Failures can become blessings in disguise. Years ago, cashews were the biggest money crop for my father at his farm. Later an attack of insects destroyed the cashew trees and the pests began to eat the crops and fruits. Farmers like him were in immense peril. Instead of lamenting over it or giving up their work and worrying about their failures, they made a wise decision to replace cashew trees with rubber trees. Soon rubber became a more profitable and reliable cash crop than cashews. They embarrassed failure and got rid of its destructive grips.

It's a myth to think that failures are undefeatable and its juggernauts are unstoppable!

Every failure can teach us something if we have the right attitude. We must bust the myth that failures are undefeatable and its juggernauts are unstoppable. If we patiently watch out, we will find alternatives emerging which might make us more successful.

Amy Purdy was a successful snowboarder at the age of 15. Everyone knew that she was destined for fame. She too dreamt of success and fame. Life seemed perfect for her.

However when she was 19 years old, tragedy struck and her dreams were shattered. She got infected with a severe flu-like symptom with a high blood infection. Her life took a detour. "She has less than a 2% chance of survival", concluded her doctors.

She soon fell into a coma and was put on life support. In the following months, she lost her spleen, kidney and both legs below the knees. She also lost hearing in her left ear. After months of intense treatment, when she came out of the hospital, with a kidney donated by her dad, she was physically and emotionally shattered.

She decided to embarrass the failure and write a new chapter in her life. She began to dream again. She dreamt of snowboarding again. People were sceptical about her dreams. But she wanted to embarrass the failure with her positive actions. This determination rewrote her life story.

Soon she became a world-class snowboarder, dancer, model, actress, designer and New York Times' bestselling author. Her book 'On My Own Two Feet: From Losing My Legs to Learning the Dance of Life', has given immense ammunition to people to succeed in life.

She won two world cup gold medals in snowboarding and won two medals in the Paralympics. The doors of possibilities were opened when she decided to defeat failure instead of failure defeating her dreams. She made a mark.

3. Immerse in Passion

Another way to improve self-esteem is to immerse in our passion. When we devote ourselves to something we do well, to something we love doing, we begin to experience a higher level of fulfilment. We have so many strengths which we possess much more than other people. Develop some of these skills and talents to express our personality. Develop a desire to make a difference in the world.

The coronavirus affected everyone; some of us got infected too. We lost our dear ones. Some lost their jobs. As a result, we fell into deep depression. Even in the midst of such hopeless and frightening situations, we still can rebuild our lives and progress in life.

Edward Munch, for example, was born with low immunity levels and survived the 1918 influenza pandemic called the Spanish flue that ruptured the confidence of the modern world. One-third of the world's population was infected while more than 50 million people succumbed to it. It was the deadliest pandemic in human history.

Edward Munch too suffered much during the outbreak. People said that he wouldn't survive. However, he decided otherwise. With his resolute determination and faith, he redirected his mind and energy and rebuilt himself to realize his dream of becoming a world-renowned artist and painter. His most famous painting, the 'Scream' was born when he was affected by the Spanish flu.

When we have the right attitude to life and situations and immerse in our passion, we foster a heaven around us. Time flies! Our esteem shoots up. We make a mark in this world.

4. Keep the Rein

Studies have shown that unrealistic expectations of parents, teachers, spouses and managers can cause poor self-esteem in people. The expectations of others weigh us down. However if their expectations are noble and are for our benefit, then we should respect them. The rein should be in our hands.

People with high self-esteem are not worried about what others think or expect. They live their lives with deep respect for others. People expect us to live well and use our maximum potential.

> What we think of ourselves is much more important than what others think about us.

I have seen on my father's farm that whenever a tree tends to bend and go in the wrong direction, he ties a rope to it, pulls it straight and ties it on a stronger tree. This helps the tree to grow tall and strong. The expectations of others, in the same way, pull us up to give our best. These good people help us to deliver our best.

At the same time, never allow others and situations to control our lives. We are the king of ourselves and only we have the authority to make us happy or sad. What we think of ourselves is much more important than what others think about us.

We shouldn't compare ourselves negatively or unrealistically. Others have their strengths. But we have our innumerable strengths too. Don't let others take the rein of our life in their hands.

As we keep the rein of our dreams in our hands, loosen it at times to visualize success the way we want. Dream about winning; dream that we will succeed in everything we do. Imagine how people will appreciate us when we reach our goals.

If we visualize success before we actually get to work then we will seldom fail. We have unlimited personal power. Use this power to win and boost confidence.

5. Live Among Angels

Live in the company of good friends and supporters who will help us to maintain our self-esteem. Build a network of supportive relationships. Good friends can boost our self-esteem. We are created to relate; are wired to connect; are called to help.

Human beings have survived the onslaught of nature, wars, terrorist attacks, famines and epidemics because of their willingness to stand together. Loners will perish. We need others. We are basically a tribal group and if we stay alone, we will experience threats from all directions. If we remain alienated, we will be defeated by the aliens.

We need the angels. Ensure to live among good people, seek their advice and we will walk the right path. Always have the company of good, self-confident people. At the same time, we must remember that we alone are responsible for what we do. Spend time with people who will appreciate and care for us. Distance the toxic and seek out the company of the positive.

"Associate with people of good quality if you esteem your reputation; for it is better to be alone than to be in bad company," says George Washington, the first President of US. Associating ourselves with people of high moral character will help us to build our self-esteem.

One of the best ways to boost one's self-esteem is to become an angel for others. This compels us to discover the true meaning of life and live with a purpose. There are far too many critics in the world and we are too often brutally wounded by them. We need to consciously avoid such tyrants. "What people in the world think about you is really none of your business", says Martha Graham, American dancer and choreographer.

I have immense admiration and love for my father who, at 85, lives a highly disciplined life, follows his to-do list meticulously and continues to perform each activity with a purpose. For example, he continues to spend his time on his farm planting areca-nut and coconut trees, knowing well he may not enjoy its fruits.

However he believes that this gives him meaning in life. He looks beyond the profit to the purpose. Can we become an angel like him and live with a purpose?

6. Love a Positive Life

When we are stuck by negative thoughts we must act like the jury, question our minds and ask for proof. If we feel that we are not good looking, not smart enough, not talented like others, then challenge the mind for proof for thinking so.

Often the mind won't be able to give any proof because these are assumptions made by it. Once we know that these are assumptions and fears, then replace these negative thoughts with positive ones.

Think of our strengths, skills and talents. Try to write down things that we can do well. Recollect the many good things we have done in the past for others. Think of the innumerable accomplishments. Realize how beautiful this life is. Think positive and love this life.

Raj my friend, has a dangler in his car with the words, 'Only Positive Vibes.' "As I drive home after a heavy day of targets, unfulfilled expectations and unrealistic bosses, whenever my mind tends to become negative, this little dangler reminds me to look at the positive part of the day. This helps me to drive with a smile", he says. Even on the toughest day when everything is cloudy and rainy we still have the power to think positive.

7. Take Care of the Self

As we said in the previous chapter, we need to take care of our whole self: physical, social, mental and spiritual if we are keen to improve our self-esteem. Living healthy, for example, can help us to build our self-esteem. Eating well, dieting, exercising, pursuing a hobby, following a proper schedule and having a to-do list can help us to uplift our spirits. These things help the brain to release endorphins that make us feel good. A healthy and sound body can enhance our self-esteem.

Sleeping well will make us feel good. Stress and anger arise from lack of sleep and bring down our self-esteem. So make sure you have sufficient time to relax and sleep.

Dancing is an excellent tool to relax. In my previous organization, we started the practice sof concluding the training with a dance. People, if they felt shy, could blindfold themselves and dance to any music to lift up their spirits and become more confident.

When we become positive and optimistic about ourselves we create a positive environment. The more we think positively about others the more positive we become.

Self-esteem is more important than good health and wealth. If we have high self-esteem, we will be successful in all that we do. We will also gain good health and wealth. We just need to be ourselves, believe in our power and success will run after us.

Life is full of ups and downs, challenges and surprises, sorrows and joys. However tough it is, there is always a silver line beyond the horizon that fills us with optimism and positivity. These positive vibes empower us to make a mark in this world.

5 Attitude Makes the Difference

We are the owners of innumerable skills, immense knowledge and imperishable talents. Though we have the best opportunities, not all of us succeed in life. With my two decades of experience as an HRDian and having trained more than 55,000 people, I realize that skills, knowledge and talents alone won't make one successful. We need them surely; but we need more a positive attitude to win the battles of life.

It is our attitude that makes us progress in our lives. It determines how high we grow in our careers. It tells how well we live our lives. It makes the difference!

I love to travel while my brother Biju is in the driver's seat. As he steers along the winding roads of my village and climbs up the mountains and drives down the steep valleys that surround my little hamlet, he remains super cool, serene, calm and composed while we sit breathlessly watching the deep valleys and dangerous terrains.

We would suddenly come across another jeep or a bike rushing from the opposite side along the small road. "I control my car and they control theirs", he would assure us. If we are in control, then the ride becomes an amazing and safe experience!

There are things over which we have no control or have very little control. But if we control our attitudes, these uncontrollable things will contribute positively to our personality.

People react differently to the same event. It's strange! And this is the result of attitude. External events may be beyond our control, but our reactions are entirely under our control. If we have the right attitude and learn to monitor and control our behaviours our lives will be a celebration.

Attitude is the way we look at the world. We can look at the world in two ways: positively or negatively. Our personality gets formed by the choice we make. Depending on this we can be the biggest asset or the biggest liability in family, society or organization. We have to manage our attitude and cultivate positivity in spite of all struggles we face daily.

> The foundation of our happiness, success and productivity is our attitude.

Can we change our attitude? Yes we can.

"The greatest discovery of my generation is that human beings can alter their lives by altering their attitudes of mind," says William James, philosopher and psychologist in his book 'The Varieties of Religious Experience.'

Great buildings have great foundations. The foundation of our happiness, success and productivity is our attitude. If I am a person of negative attitude, I can choose to become a positive person. It's possible though not easy. No one lives forever in a gutter unless he decides to do so. We have the power and the opportunity to get up, shake the dirt off and walk on.

Think Positive to Become Positive

Thinking is the key to alter the attitude. If we change our thinking, our perspective changes. Hence to change our attitude, we must learn to think positively whenever something negative happens to us.

Try to see something good in every person and in every event. Speak positively about yourself and others. Fill the minds with more positive thoughts than negative ones. Think 'I can' and you will succeed. Learn to look more at the half-full glass and forget about the half-empty glass; you will see life in full everywhere. Think positive to become positive.

If we possess the right attitude, we will stop searching for diamonds elsewhere. Rather, if we have the right attitude we will realize that we are walking on diamonds.

We see in every event and in every person a great opportunity to learn and grow. We will be optimistic and see only good in everyone and everywhere; then, we will begin to count our many blessings instead of our few failures.

With the right attitude, every failure becomes an opportunity to learn. Positive attitude enables us to walk towards success with greater determination and passion.

Our environment, education and experience can determine our attitude. Our attitude is the core of our humanness. Irrespective of the environment, upbringing, genetics and political pressures, we still have the privilege of choosing the right attitude. This is the beauty of human nature. No one can take away this privilege from us. "Everything can be taken away, but not our attitude," says Viktor Frankl, the author of 'Man's Search for Meaning'.

Environmental factors like our homes, schools, friends, workplaces, media, cultural, religious, social, and political situations can mould our attitude. The positive experience we have of a person, an event or a situation also gives us a positive attitude. Wisdom, knowledge, skills and experience also can determine our attitude.

More than all these, what we think we become. We need to consciously choose to think positive to acquire the right attitude.

What is the Colour of Your Spectacles?

Our attitude is like the spectacle we wear. If our glasses are red, we tend to see everything red. If it's blue, green or pink, we see accordingly. Though the external reality remains the same, we see it differently because of the attitude with which we perceive it.

Do you remember the fable of the mouse that became a lion? The mouse was so unhappy with himself that he wanted to become someone big. He lived with a low self-concept and a negative attitude. He lived in a gutter where he was being constantly chased by a cat. He was getting depressed day by day. "Only if I become a cat will I be happy," he told himself.

He went to a guru who possessed magical powers and begged him to transform him into a cat. The guru felt compassion and changed the mouse into a cat. The rat was delighted and ran around proudly frightening his fellow mice.

After a few days, he found that he was being chased by a dog. He became scared of the dog and said, "Only if I could become like a dog will I be happy." So he went to the guru with a new request.

The good guru obliged and transformed him into a dog. With his ferocious barks, he could now scare the cats away. He was proud of himself and was happy with his new status.

But soon he realized he was being chased by a lion who was searching for its prey. "If I become a lion, I will be the king of the jungle and everyone will respect me," he said to himself.

The guru accepted his request again and made him a lion. He lived like a king for some days. One day as he was on a royal tour around the jungle, he found some men laying a trap to capture the lion. They wanted the lion to be caged in a zoo. He became scared of these men, ran to the guru and told him to make him a man.

The guru, after a profound thought, said, "Nothing will help you unless you change your attitude. Though outwardly you are a lion, you still possess the heart of a mouse. Your titles, status, power, might, privileges or wealth will not make you a lion or a man."

So the guru pronounced his magical words and transformed him into a mouse again.

I might be on the top of the hierarchy, possess immense wealth, command hundreds of people, have excellent titles, status and power, but without a positive attitude, all these are vanity. If our attitude is negative we will continue to live with the heart of a mouse in the gutter. We must change our attitude not the titles or the jobs.

Fruits of Positive Attitude

"The success or failure of any work depends on the mindset and attitude of the person doing the work", says Chung Ju Yung, the legendary founder of Hyundai. He believed that skills are teachable if the attitude is good. No wonder today many organizations view attitude as one of the critical traits in their hiring processes.

Like an apple tree that gives an abundance of fruits, our attitude too gives us a variety of fruits! The fruits of positive attitude are like the sands on the seashore. The wise use it to make a difference.

A person with a positive attitude is caring, confident, patient, humble, cheerful, fun-loving, hardworking, dedicated, committed and has high expectations about himself and others. He constantly improves his productivity, has an easy approach to problems, improves the quality of work and creates lasting and effective relationships. He is highly loyal to the organization, passionately contributes to its profit, has a pleasing personality, is courageous to take risks and initiatives, and takes responsibility for his growth and performance.

On the other hand, a negative attitude can ruin a person's career and life. As a result, one becomes bitter, resentful and a pessimist. It has awful effects on one's health, relationships and performance. Such people constantly complain that roses have thorns and fail to see the beautiful roses among the thorns.

Attitude affects every aspect of life. Happiness is the product of attitude because the right attitude will produce the right actions. Only the right actions can make us happy. If we have the right attitude, we will see the invisible, feel the intangible and achieve the impossible. Having positive attitude is a sure way to succeed in life. It is a sure way to a long, healthy and cheerful life.

> If we have the right attitude we will see the invisible, feel the intangible and achieve the impossible.

Our attitude gives us the power and the push to become what we are capable of. A travelling painter once reached a small town looking for models to paint. A drunk approached him and asked him to paint his picture. He was shabby, untidy, unshaven and fully drunk. The artist started to draw and once the picture was ready showed the portrait to the drunk.

"This is not me", said the drunkard as he stared at the handsome, smiling and enthusiastic young man in the portrait.

"This is who you really are", answered the painter.

He saw beneath the external appearance of the drunkard and understood what he could become. His attitude, inner beauty and dignity were hidden from the sight of others.

"This is the person you can become", the painter told the drunkard. "Alter your attitude to become a positive and charming personality", he said.

Darkness Travels Faster Than the Light

Negativism spreads like a virus. It is the fastest in the world. Good takes time; it is damn slow. "No matter how fast light travels, it finds that darkness has always got there and is waiting for it", says Terry Pratchett, the best-selling author of fantasy stories.

Living with pessimism is so natural to us while optimism consumes a lot of effort. It's easy to talk bad about others; to talk positive, we need a lot of energy and effort.

Some people love darkness while some are scared of it. I have met people who are afraid of the light. They prefer to stay in darkness, enslaved by negativism, bias and prejudice.

"The real tragedy of life is when people are afraid of the light", says Plato. These people miss the beautiful dawn and the warmth of the rising sun. They are unwilling to light their lanterns and don't realize that positivism can dispel the darkness in their hearts.

When we have a positive attitude and live among those who are positive, we paint a positive portrait of ourselves.

Positive attitude will tell us what we can become and can help us on our journey to reach that destination.

Our attitude makes us an asset or a liability. "In life it doesn't matter if you're smart or right. What matters is that you make a positive difference in people's lives", says Marshal Goldsmith, author and leadership coach. Our attitude should make a difference both for ourselves and for the world.

Shall we sculpt our lives by chiseling away the rough edges of pessimism and negativity?

Then we will live like an asset and make a difference in this world.

6

Come Up Here!

Life is a journey of continuous ascension and descension to become better daily. We all dream to become better and better and make step by step improvements towards our goals. A few listen to the inner voice that invites them to 'come up here' and become what they are made for. They step up and go up to reach their full potential. This is what people are created for. This gives them meaning in life.

What holds us back?

Rise up to reach a higher level of life: in status, rank and quality of life. Dr. B.R. Ambedkar, the father of the Indian Constitution, is one of the best role models for anyone who aspires to go up in life.

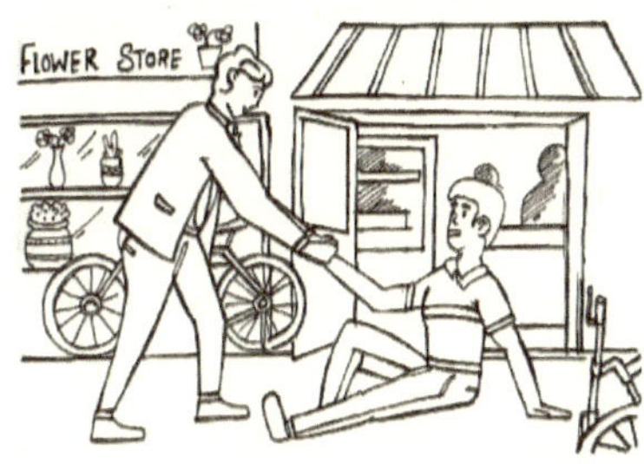

Though his father was an army officer, because he was from a low caste, he tasted humiliation and oppression as a student. He was not permitted to sit with his classmates; was given a special seat outside the classroom; was not permitted to drink water from the same vessel; was not permitted to speak or mingle with other students. Though he educated himself well with the support of some benefactors, he failed to get a decent job as he was an 'untouchable'.

As a pioneering leader with a distinct love for his people, he decided to stand up and speak up for the Dalits and fight against discrimination and untouchability. As a social reformer, he helped many downtrodden to come up in life. Through his writings, he brought hope to millions of people and inspired them to come up to a higher status in life.

He gave them hope and the opportunity to achieve their dreams. He told them what they were capable of and what they could achieve against all odds they faced. He became a legend because he listened to his inner voice that urged him to 'come up here'. He exhorted his people to listen to this voice too.

Listen to the Voice: 'Come Up Here'

The doors are open for us to enter a world of complete magnificence. The previous chapters of this book helped us to become aware of ourselves and showcased the right personality traits. We have acquired a higher level of self-esteem and identified ways to become more positive in life. We are now ready to go up to a higher orbit of life!

We have heard many stories about people who have listened to the inner voice and transformed their lives. Emily Blunt is one such hero. Though she was fortunate to have been born into an affluent and influential family she suffered from stuttering as a young girl.

Communication was a self-defeating experience for her as she would stammer every word she uttered. She felt crippled in the presence of others and could not convey what she thought. It diminished her self-esteem.

She received a good education, possessed a smart outlook and formed the right perspective on life but was incapable of communicating her views convincingly. Stammering became a huge challenge to achieve her goals. As she feared public speaking and meeting people, she began to withdraw and live a lonely life.

While in school, one of her teachers helped her to overcome this fear. She asked Emily to join the acting classes which she gently refused because of fear. However, the teacher would continue to encourage and motivate her to take up acting classes. Finally she won and the faith the teacher had in Emily brought her many laurels in life including the Golden Globe Award.

In the same way, the doors of success are open for each one of us. We only need to look at our potential and listen to the inner voice: 'come up here.' If we give up those things that prevent us from going up, we experience magnificence!

Give Up to Go Up

We are pulled down by the gravitational force of our desires, lust, selfishness and pride. If we wish to go up, we must give up first. Wash away the past; don't rely on things that made us successful or continue to do what we did best in the past.

Many cultures and traditions ask people to remove their shoes as they enter their homes or places of worship. For example, in Holy Bible, Yahweh tells Moses at Mount Sinai, "If you want to come up here, remove your shoes, for the place where you stand is holy."

> "If you want to come up here, remove your shoes, for the place where you stand is holy."
> Holy Bible

Sinai was a place of holiness; to enter that place one had to give up the dirt of the past that one had been carrying all along. Removing shoes was a sign of forfeiting the comforts of the past, becoming humble and showing respect. He was asked to remove his past: his skills, knowledge and experience that made him a leader. He was asked to up-skill and reskill himself to reach a higher status of life. He was asked to give up to go up!

Thus, the first step to go up is to unglue ourselves from the past. Our past weighs us down. We are chained to the past as it fills us with pride, fear or shame. Of course, we need to learn from the past but the past has to go. Give it up to go up.

Are we ready to let go of the many successes, the pains and the wounds of the past? Our potential self is shouting out to us to 'come up here' while our current self is down in the gutter struggling to stand up. What made us succeed in the past will not take us to our goals in future.

We are caught up with too many things. The Greek word 'harpazo' explains our nature too well. It means 'caught up and ruptured'. We are caught up and raptured in the web of our desires which snatches our energy and life. We are gripped and forcibly put in a prison of our desires and bodily lust, pride, ego, selfishness and greed. Listen urgently to the voice 'come up here', give up the many things that pull us down and go up to live a happier life.

Identify the things that pull you down. Create an action plan to give them up. Work daily to go up step by step. If you want to fly, give up everything that weighs you down.

The Risk of the Trapeze Artist

As children, my sisters, brother and I would eagerly wait for the annual temple festival in our village. It would

be an added bonus after Christmas and the New Year as numerous shops, stalls and stages would mushroom in the vast playgrounds of the temple.

My otherwise remote and unknown little hamlet, surrounded by green mountains, caressed by cold breezes and showered by heavy rains, would suddenly come alive and bustling with thousands of people visiting the temple to celebrate the festival.

We would almost worship the heroism of the bikers, who would show us stunning tricks inside the 'death-well'. We would be fans of the numerous magicians, the acrobats and the giant wheels and continue to retell and reenact their stories even for months after the festival.

However the most attractive item of course would be the circus. It was an annual ritual for many families to watch the circus. We would hold our breaths as the artists displayed terrific performances.

One of the most memorable items in the circus, even after so many years, is the performance of the beautiful trapeze artists in glittering dresses. They would be in the sky most of the time, jumping from one bar to another, as the people below watched them with huge applause.

Jiny, my younger sister, would be scared of the trapeze acts and would cling to my mother tight. She didn't want the artists to leave their hands from the bar for fear of falling. "Only by taking the risk of letting go of their aerial bars or ropes would they be able to create a magical performance", my mother would console her.

They could reach the next bar or the ropes or into the hands of another trapeze artist only if they decided to leave the bar on which they were hanging. They would swing, fly and create marvels in the sky by leaving their comfort zones and flying to the next trapeze. The audience would be in awe with excitement, clap their hands and appreciate the excellent performance.

The magic would happen only if the artist decided to leave her hands from the trapeze bar.

How often do we hold on to the bar and refuse to let it go? Are we scared of losing our reputation by taking risks?

"When Henry Ford made cheap reliable cars, people said: 'what's wrong with a horse", says Elon Musk. Ford took a risk and it worked! Excellence comes only to those willing to give up, let go of the past and take the risk of flying into the unknown like a trapeze artist.

'Come Up Here' to a Better Place

Complacency is evil. Human nature is progressive and wants to move on from what it is today to a better place. Everyone wants to move towards something ideal, a place better than where he is today. We look up to become more powerful and more successful to live a more vibrant, happy and contented life. We want to go up to become happy.

> Complacency is evil. Human nature is progressive and wants to move on from what it is today to a better place.

The Book of Revelation in the Holy Bible discusses the concept of 'come up here.' St. John, the author, narrates a vision that he had. "I saw an open door and heard a voice that sounded like a trumpet, telling 'come up here." John, through the open door, is taken to the presence of the divine and is transformed by this beatific vision.

He lived on the island of Patmos which was a barren volcanic island in the Aegean Sea. The island which was 10 miles long, 6 miles wide and 40 miles off the shore of Miletus, was commonly used as a prison or as a place to which people were exiled. He received the invitation to 'come up here' while he was in that prison.

Are we not imprisoned? Imprisoned by our past, pride, selfishness, low self-esteem and low self-confidence? We possess immense treasures of talents, potentials, capabilities and strengths but live pathetic lives as a prisoner of our ego, attitude and ignorance at the Patmos of our mindset.

Patmos represents the present life we lead. We are questioned by our inner self as it struggles to go up. In this world of Patmos, we experience suffering, imperfection, misunderstandings, conflicts, isolation, pain, rejection, disrespect and hatred. We are in deep pain. We feel isolated, abandoned, rejected and unfairly treated. We constantly seek for a better place of happiness and peace. In the midst of all these, we wait for an external miraculous power to come to our aid.

Instead we should believe in our inner strength. When the inner voice says 'come up here', rely on this voice and take the initiatives to go up in life. Nothing else will bail us out of this gutter of Patmos except our determination to follow the dictum 'come up here.' No emperors, no powers, no wealth, no status and no other being can help us in this movement. When we decide to go up, it just happens!

Have you not heard the voice of the trumpet, 'come up here'? We hear it often but we ignore it. We know what is right and wrong, what is good and bad, what is virtuous and vice. However we choose the easy path not the right path. Between the easy and the tough, the mediocre choose the easy while the successful choose the tough.

> We know what is right and wrong, what is good and bad, what is virtuous and vice. However we choose the easy path not the right path.

What happened to John when he went up? He saw "A throne and someone sitting on it." We are filled with our ego. This ego makes us feel proud, important and arrogant. However to go up we must give up this urge to become important. There is someone else sitting on the throne. We need to be humble.

Suppose we are at a wedding reception and as we stand among the crowd for our turn to reach the stage to greet the couple, the host from the stage suddenly calls out our name and says 'come up here.' How do we feel? We feel elated and important in front of other guests. But to receive that invitation, we must be among the crowd first with all humility and selflessness.

As we are escorted onto the stage, we begin to wonder whether the gift we brought to give to the couple is worthy enough for this special invitation to 'come up here.' We often feel we are unprepared, don't have the best gift and are unqualified for that invitation.

The popular talk show 'The Les Brown Show', is hosted by Les Brown. However his life is a story of rags to riches. From the gutters of his destitute self-esteem and disadvantageous life, he listened to the voice 'come up here.'

Born in an impoverished Miami family, he endured the bitterness of hardship and struggles. He was also considered a dull student in school and was even nicknamed 'mentally handicapped.' His teachers de-promoted him because of poor scores and labelled him dumb and stupid.

One of his teachers who had a soft corner for him and believed in him, asked him one day to solve a problem. He declined saying he was a dull student. The teacher, however, went on to encourage him to think of himself differently.

While the whole class laughed at him, his teacher gave him confidence. "You are capable of doing better Les", she said. "Come up here. The opinions of others do not limit your boundaries", she would encourage.

Believing her words, he picked up courage and defeated the incredible odds he faced in life not only on that day but all through his life. He pursued his goal passionately and went on to become one of the most renowned motivational speakers and a member of the Ohio House of Representatives.

'Come Up Here' to Build the Right Perspective

"Life is full of battles. Fight to the last without fear, stand your ground", says the Bhagavad Gita. Desires for results and expectations fill us with fear and pull us down. We want results; we have expectations; we struggle to fulfil the expectations of others. Though desires are natural and humane, we either suppress them or allow them to control us. Both are wrong.

> "Life is full of battles. Fight to the last without fear, stand your ground."
> Bhagavad Gita

The Bhagavad Gita teaches us to let the desire for results and expectations come and pass through us, but we are to remain like a spectator to build up the right perspectives in life.

The Kurukshetra war was imminent and the best warrior of Pandavas was baffled, confused, dejected and afraid. Arjuna refused to engage in the war fully. He was proficient in his role but failed to have a proper perspective on war, life and death. He was confronted by the desire for results. Desires destroy life.

Lord Krishna helped him to sieve the right perspective and that made him a better warrior and a better human being. Krishna gave him the right perspective and opened the doors to enter a new and better world of detachment.

I once asked a colleague why he kept a statue of Lord Ganesha at the gate of his home. He gave me an interesting answer.

According to faith, Ganesha is the guardian of every home. He watches the gates to protect the house. He keeps away negativity, self-doubt, deception, excessive desires, pride and arrogance not only from our homes but also from our hearts. He guards and directs the perceptions of people who live there. He helps in 'Pratyahara', to withdraw from our senses and go deep into ourselves to realize the positive energy.

This positive energy closes the gates of perception. Once the doors of perceptions are closed, the doors to bliss and wisdom open. Then we hear the voice, 'come up here.'

Shivaji Rao Gaikward comes from an ordinary family. He lost his mother when he was five; worked as a coolie, a carpenter and as a bus conductor to support his family. One day as he was on duty as a conductor, he saw an advertisement about an acting school. But he had no money.

When his close friend heard about his goal, he agreed to finance him. Later a prominent Tamil film director gave him a petite role in his film. Shivaji went on to create history and became the heartthrob of the Indian film industry as Superstar Rajni Kanth. His friends and well-wishers supported him to listen to his inner voice, 'come up here'. Similarly life gives super stardom to those who listen to their inner voice.

'Come Up Here' to Discover Hope

Oftentimes, we live a life of hopelessness. But with hope we become different and new. "Hope is being able to see that there is light despite all the darkness", says Desmond Tutu, the African bishop and human rights activist. It gives us the optimism to look at the open door. There is a new world of happiness beyond the door. It's up to us to get up and come up to enter the door.

One of the most unpleasant experiences I have had while travelling in buses in Kerala, the southern state of India, is the encounters that I have with people who sell lotteries. They pester, plead, threaten or curse till you buy. They place the ticket on your lap, put it in your pocket or push it into your hands. They sell hope at first, the hope of winning a prize. Then they seek sympathy from you and request you to buy. Finally they even threaten you with an imminent danger if you don't comply.

> Though we possess innumerable talents, we hide them to live unproductive and unhappy lives and depart from this world, leaving no footprints on the sands of time.

The lottery sellers thrive because ultimately they succeed in convincing some travellers who travel in search of hope. So far in life, I have never met anyone who won the lottery. Even those who buy the lottery know that their chance of winning is very remote. Yet people buy. The lottery industry is one of the most profitable businesses. They are successful because they sell hope. People buy hopping they will become rich someday. They hope for a better future.

The promise 'come up here' is not a lottery. Instead we have the complete assurance of success if we take the first step to go up and enter through the door. Hope inspires us to take the steps to become prosperous.

When you hear the voice 'come up here' abandon your past and go up confidently to enter into a new glorious world of immense possibilities where you can unleash your potential and realize your dreams.

"Come up here and I will show you the things which must take place after this", says the Book of Revelation. But alas, we have become complacent with our existing environment. We carry with us a lukewarm attitude to our immense potential. Though we possess innumerable talents, we hide them to live unproductive and unhappy lives and depart from this world, leaving no footprints on the sands of time.

Rise from the Gutters

Everyone experiences the stench, the chill and the darkness of the gutters. Some even get killed inside the gutter. The gutter refers to a physical illness, a financial loss, emotional turbulence or a relationship breakage. We become drenched, dirty and stinking. We feel disconnected, distanced, defeated and in danger while in the gutter. Our pessimism becomes louder than the inner voice 'Come Up Here'.

If we are lucky enough, we will have amazing angels coming on our way to save us from the gutters of life. I remember Dr. Joe Almeida as an affectionate superior and mentor who has been the face of goodness and  gentleness for me and for many like me who experienced the gutters. His optimism, healing words, forgiving attitude and reassuring presence have helped me to come up from many highly challenging situations.

He believed in the possibilities to become better and always gave another chance when we made mistakes. He, with his loving kindness and caring gestures, made us realize the wrong decisions we made and encouraged us to push ourselves up from the gutters.

We construct our gutters brick by brick through our wrongful acts and habits, through our indiscipline and lack of self-control. Vices give us an easy and slippery path. Gutters ruin our character and reputation. But we list numerous justifications for being in the gutter.

> "A person without self-control is like a city that is broken into and left without walls."
>
> Holy Bible

He gave me light. He invited me to spread the light instead of living in darkness. He lit my lantern and helped me to rise up from the gutters. "A person without self-control is like a city that is broken into and left without walls", says the Holy Bible.

Courage or Comfort

Brian Cavanaugh, in his book the Sower's Seeds, narrates an inspiring fable of a beautiful bird. He was free, bold, fearless and brave. He would fly to distant places and would go high up in the sky just for pleasure.

However he became proud when the other birds began to admire him. So one day, he decided to construct a beautiful nest for himself to gain more admiration from others. He began to pluck his feathers one by one to make the nest where he could sit comfortably. Finally when the nest was ready, the bird could no longer fly!

We need to give up comfort to go up. This takes courage. Unfortunately many of us love to remain in the gutters of life even though the doors are open. We blame others for our inaction. We ignore the invitation to 'come up here'. We live inside the little boxes of complacency and comfort and are unwilling to go out.

It's painful to leave the familiar shores. We become anxious to move out of our comfort zones and are unwilling to fly out.

It's tough and painful. But if we move, we will discover a whole new world of opportunities. To move is the best decision one can take.

The door that St. John saw was an open door. It was a door to a more prosperous life. It was a door to a panorama of possibilities. The doors are accessible even today for those who are willing to go up.

Those who choose to enter through the door, live in the garden of goodness and breathe the fragrance of success. They live their lives fully, become legendary and dedicate their lives to make legends. They chronicle success in all its hues and colours, spread hope and walk confidently in the midst of the tremors and turpitudes of life.

Light your lantern! The doors are open. Take the first step and walk ahead. What are we waiting for?

Skill, Wisdom or Goodness

"The sage asked the spirit of wisdom thus:
'Is wisdom good or skill or goodness?'

The spirit of wisdom answered thus:
'Wisdom with which there is no goodness is not wisdom;
skill with which there is no wisdom is not skill either."

Pahlavi Texts

<table><tr><td>**1**</td><td>

Learn More, Grow More

</td></tr></table>

Knowledge is the key to growth and prosperity. "A person who graduates today and stops learning tomorrow is illiterate the day after", says Newton D Baker, US politician and lawyer. In today's fast-changing world, to make oneself relevant, agile and successful one has to go on learning. The moment we stop learning, we stop growing; and we stop earning!

We never fail in life. We either earn or learn. "Don't ask what will happen if we train people and they leave; instead, ask what will happen if we don't train people and they stay on", says Zig Ziglar, the motivational guru. Many organizations invest heavily in employee training and development.

Learning has become a vital part of every HR activity helping employees cope with the changes in digital, functional, technical and behavioural sciences. Chung Ju Yung, the founder of Hyundai says, "In today's competitive market, what will make you succeed is the presence of highly motivated and highly trained employees."

Learning helps one to remain young. It constantly challenges one's mind and these challenges will generate rambunctiousness and excitement to live a life of youthfulness and dynamism irrespective of one's age.

Do you wish to remain young?

Here are some ways to remain young and grow up gracefully.

1. Have a Dream

We are what we are because of our dreams. The moment we lose our dreams, we die. Dreams and goals give us energy, enthusiasm, direction, purpose and meaning. We need to struggle hard to realize these dreams and this struggle is delicious. Success without struggles challenges nobody.

However achieving a particular goal doesn't mean we have fully grown. We have to set new goals and push ourselves to achieve higher ones. We must constantly strive to grow, learn and perfect our talents to achieve these goals.

We set a lot of goals. What are our learning goals? What did we learn in the last one month?

Learning makes us visionary. George Cadbury in 1920s believed that a more educated, healthier, happier and cleaner employee was an asset to the organization. He went on to construct a training centre, not only for his employees but also for their spouses and children because he said a more educated employee would contribute better to the company. He started a gym in the vicinity of his factory because he believed that a healthier employee could be an asset. He knew that frequent absenteeism due to illness would affect his company's growth.

He constructed a swimming pool in the middle of his factory. Why? Because he said "A cleaner employee is a brand ambassador for me. When my customers see my employees coming out of the factory spotless, smart and well dressed, they will trust the quality, hygiene and safety of my products."

Learning gives us the inspiration, energy, skills and tools to construct dreams step by step till we achieve them. It infuses the thirst to become better every day. It propels us to visualize a more beautiful place as our destination.

2. Have the Desire

We need to have strong will power and desire to grow and learn from all situations. If we have the will to learn and grow we are bound to succeed. When we have this will to learn, we will broaden our mental perception, widen our horizons of imagination, enlarge our worldview and begin to do incredible things, surprising not only others but even ourselves.

> If we are afraid of mistakes, we will never grow. Challenges charge us and help us grow.

"Have the courage to do new things if you want to learn and grow", I remind my participants. I exhort them to take up initiatives and risks. Fear of failure can prevent us from venturing into newer and deeper oceans. Boost the willpower to face the violent waves for we learn more by making mistakes.

Children fall many times before they learn to walk. Failures do not deter them from taking the next step. If we are afraid of mistakes, we will never grow. Challenges charge us and help us grow.

We need to cultivate the will and the desire to learn constantly. We don't know everything. There are plenty of things yet to learn. The moment we feel self-sufficient and satisfied with our knowledge and talents we fail to grow.

Also admit the mistakes gracefully and apologize promptly instead of becoming defensive and blaming others for our failures. Arrogant self-satisfaction and pride are great walls that prevent learning and growing.

Have a teachable attitude with a fire to learn; and you are on the way to success. This desire for knowledge determines the destiny.

3. Have Fun

Learning is faster in the presence of fun. We learnt better as kids because our teachers taught us using rhymes, stories, pictures and toys. We must learn to laugh and find humour every day and everywhere. Enjoy learning from everyone and from all situations.

An optimistic, happy, hilarious and fun loving person is a fast learner. He will find opportunities everywhere for learning. Even the worst situation can be an occasion for learning and growing.

Not only children even adults learn with fun. Learning shouldn't be funny but should be with fun. When trainers design their learning curriculum, they need to create a course keeping in mind the different types of learners: auditory, visual and kinesthetic. Every teacher and trainer should gain ample knowledge on the theories of adult learning and the theory of multiple intelligences.

Andragogy is not just a transfer of knowledge. Knowledge gained by an adult should be usable. The adult learner while learning goes through four stages: Receive, Assimilate, Store and Use. When these stages are colored with fun in a non-threatening context, learning becomes exciting and valuable.

4. Have Freedom

Adult learning is democratic. The adult learner should have the freedom to choose what he wants to learn. He knows what is best for him. The learning should help him to bridge the gap in his skill and performance. Sometimes we deliver excellent trainings but are void of any results. This is because our programs are not based on the need of the participants. Instead of pushing our agenda, the participants should be allowed to select from an ala carte.

When trainers liberate themselves from their past successes and design the courses to suit the need of the trainees they will become like a good doctor who diagnoses the illness better and gives the right medicine to heal.

Nothing can enslave one more than past successes. The moment we become happy with our past achievements and successes we cease to grow. Use past successes to push toward future goals. Future successes will demand from us more preparation, more learning and more dedication.

We must learn to cannibalize the past successes so that new ones relevant for today will arise. When we come out of the comfort zones of past successes we see light beyond the horizon. This will rupture the way we think, behave, relate and live. It will make us better.

The successful past of ours is forgotten by everyone in the world except us. The past is no guarantee that our future is going to be brighter unless we continue to learn and grow. Break the chains of the past and embrace the present by gaining knowledge on new technology and developing capabilities for the future. Freedom from the past is essential to learn new things.

5. Have No Regrets

We don't need to regret either. Regrets pull us down in our journey of learning and growing. Use every moment to learn and grow but never have any regrets in life except for the opportunities we lost to learn. Have no regrets because we failed to change the systems and teach others; be glad you learnt something in the meantime.

I remind my participants that they need to invest more in their learning ability and not in earning ability alone. If we take care of the first, even if we lose our jobs, wealth or business, we can regain everything because we have invested in our learning ability. We must invest on our learning to earn more.

The recent floods and landslides in Kerala devastated not only properties of people but also their dreams. Ashok like many others, lost everything. But he was cool and calm unlike the others. While the rest had invested their money in consumer goods, in large houses and properties, Ashok took the wise decision to invest in his learning. "I lost my assets. But I have my earning ability", he said confidently.

"Learning is a treasure that accompanies its owner everywhere." Our success is the result of our ability to learn and grow in all situations. Harold Geneen, a business leader once noted, "In the business world, everyone is paid in two coins: cash and experience. Take the experience first; the cash will come later."

Look at the job as the best time to build our experience. Take up additional tasks to sharpen the skills. Immerse into jobs other than the KPIs to broaden the horizons of learning. Treat life itself as an opportunity to learn and grow, not just to earn and grow.

A Noble Profession

I am indebted to my gurus who inspired me to take up the call of becoming a trainer. It is a profession both challenging and fulfilling. It compels me to learn daily.

Trainers are not merely facilitators. They are influencers and nurturers. This is the reason why trainers become a popular league in any organization. As a trainer, I had excellent opportunities to influence the career and the lives of people. The trainers play a significant role in the life of every participant.

I have had hundreds of fulfilling experiences while listening to stories from participants especially from the new joiners. For the new joiners, the trainer they meet during the induction training is the face of the organization. His influence is beyond measure. He is a big hero and they will always hold him in the highest esteem. They will remember him for life.

This happens not because a trainer's job is merely a show business but because of the influence he exerts. This happens because he continuously improves himself to gain more wisdom and power to touch the hearts of his participants. This happens because his heart is ruled by goodness, love and compassion. A trainer's job is not an eight-to-six job; it is lifelong. It is noble!

Learning Leads to Prosperity

Do you want to become prosperous in life? Become a learner. "Human beings have the right to be free and prosperous. Education is the best route to achieve these things", says Fukuzawa Yukichi, educator and economist who played a prominent role in the modernization and economic prosperity of Japan. He encouraged people to work for national prosperity instead of individual prosperity. Learning ensures prosperity.

Learning should fit the needs between an organization and its employees. Chris Argyris, the developer of the theory of 'action science', pioneered the concept of Knowledge Management to bring prosperity to organizations and their people. He felt that the incongruence between the needs and goals of the organization and the employees can be bridged by making knowledge actionable.

"Successful companies create and use knowledge as a source of competitive advantage", says Nonaka Ikujiro, in his book, 'The Knowledge Creating Company'. Learning, self-renewal and prosperity are linked to each other. Organizations that do not learn will perish. So too people!

"In a hierarchy, every employee tends to rise to the level of his own incompetence", says Lawrence Peter the proposer of Peter Principle. Hence knowledge should be actionable. People should use it to create a better place.

Prosperity includes more than material prosperity. Learning gives other prosperities like, peace, happiness, enlightenment, joy and empathy. It offers the learner self-confidence, self-reliance and self-regulation. These are the intangible benefits of learning.

Workplace: the Best Place to Learn

"Workplace must be a place for one's development and growth, not for earning money", says Chung Ju Yung. His story is one of fierce determination, rocklike willpower and continuous learning.

Born poor in a farming village called Asan-ri, he was an optimist who saw numerous possibilities to learn and build himself amidst the struggles he faced. He experienced the ravages of poverty, war, conflicts and political uncertainties. He used every ounce of these harsh experiences to learn and grow.

> The priest finds God in the fire; the ascetic finds God in the heart; the illiterate finds God in books and rituals; the believer finds God in the places of worship; the wise finds God in every being.

Whenever he started a new business, from shipping to construction, from steel to automobiles, his detractors questioned his capabilities. But he proved them wrong with his tenacity, visionary outlook, leadership skills and learnability. When they said, for example, that he had no experience in shipbuilding, he went on to construct the largest shipyard in the world in three years' time.

The project time fixed was five years. Ships made by Hyundai were on voyage from his port in less than three years!

He believed that if people were willing to take risks and learn from mistakes, anything was possible.

Workplace learning motivates people and helps them to gain skills and expertise to perform present and future tasks. Many of us experience a gap between what we know and what we do.

Organizations that help employees bridge this gap through formal, on the job, mentoring or shadowing programs gain massively. They foster a learning culture and reward employees who learn the best. We need to look at the workplace as a place to learn not a place to earn.

As we said, learning keeps the learner young. So the best way to remain young is to keep learning.

The Greek gods like Apollo and Aphrodite were forever young because they ate ambrosia and drank nectar. We are not gods anyway. Learning is the nectar for us mortals to remain young.

If we rest, we rust. Organizations don't want a rusted employee.

Bhagavad Gita says, "The learned finds God everywhere." The priest finds God in the fire; the ascetic finds God in the heart; the illiterate finds God in books and rituals; the believer finds God in the places of worship; the wise finds God in every being.

<table><tr><td>2</td><td>

Don't Just Sharpen the Axe; Buy A New One

</td></tr></table>

Disruptions rule the world and they accelerate human progress faster than anyone can comprehend. We live in a digitalized world that has intelligently brought together the digital and the physical world. We need to be metaversatile; no more versatile! The metaverse converges both the physical and virtual realities of life. As a result we are not only connected to other humans but also to things around us.

These disruptions have transformed every facet of humanity.

Massive transformations are imminent in the near future too. Scientists say that billions of things will be connected to the internet and even we humans will be part of this digital ubiquity. Are we prepared for this future of work?

Disruptions happen at an alarming speed. For example, in the early 80's when telephone was a luxury, as we didn't have one at home, my mother would travel more than 10 miles to my sister's home to make a call to me. However luxuries like these have become a necessity today. Almost everyone possesses a smart phone.

People have adapted to the technological revolution with high speed and loyalty. If telephone took 75 years to reach 50 million people and television took 13 years, for internet it was just four years. For ChatGPT, just a few months! Of course the world has come closer because of these remarkable innovations.

Skills are Transitory

Marathon races are part of every sporting event. Marathon tells the story of a dispatch rider called Pheidippides who was part of the Athenian army. When the Persians landed at Marathon in 490 BC, he ran to Sparta covering a distance of 149 miles to request the king of Sparta for help. It is said that he covered the distance within a day.

The Spartans were a petite army of 10,000 men while the Persians had 25,000 giving them a clear advantage in the war. The king of Sparta declined the request as they were in the midst of Carnea, their national festival and engaging in war was forbidden during the festivals.

All the soldiers were at Marathon, which was 24 miles away from Athens. The Persians divided themselves into two troops. One reached Marathon to fight the Athenians and the other went to Athens to take control of the city. The Athenian army immediately seized this opportunity and defeated the Persian army at Marathon.

Now that they had won the battle, they had to rush to Athens to protect the city from the second troop of the Persians. But someone had to run fast to Athens to tell the king that they had won the war. Pheidippides ran again and after having given the news he collapsed and died.

Dispatch riders like Pheidippides were part of every army from time immemorial. Even during the World War, since radios were not common and reliable, the army used dispatch riders to courier messages from the battlefield to the headquarters. Though it was a highly paid and highly respectable role, the advancement of technology killed this profession.

Similarly, the future of work is going to kill many professions. Jobs like a lumberjack, travel agents, postmen, book peddlers etc. are no longer in existence today. When the world is changing with such a volcanic magnitude, how are we preparing ourselves?

Management gurus draw a drastic and scary picture of the future of work. HR professionals are preparing the workforce to meet the challenges of the future that are already present at the moment. They suggest that to work differently and embrace the challenges of the future, one must learn differently. It is important to up-skill and reskill oneself so that one is part of this transformative journey.

Sharpen the Axe or Buy a New Axe?

While attending a Certification on Storytelling by Storytelling Education Arts India Council (SEAIC) my faculty narrated an inspiring story. Two woodcutters went into the forest to cut the trees, one on each side of a river. While the one on the eastern side worked hard from morning till evening and collected a good pile of wood, he felt a sense of pride as he couldn't hear any sound of the axe from the other side of the river.

"That lazy guy must be resting", he told himself as he worked hard. However now and then, he could hear the sound of the axe for a few minutes and then there would be a long stretch of silence.

At the end of the day, the woodcutter from the eastern side placed his wood on his donkey and walked proudly to the western side of the river. When he reached, to his utter shock, he saw the other man resting happily near a massive pile of wood.

"How did you achieve this? I didn't hear you work. I thought you were lazy and resting all the while", said the first.

"I didn't rest", replied the other. "I took time off to sharpen my axe. I would cut the trees for an hour and then spend time sharpening the axe. I was able to cut more trees because I spent more time sharpening my axe."

Traditional workers have been like the first woodcutter. They worked hard from morning to evening, abiding by the schedule, rules and regulations given by the organization. The second guy represents the smart worker. He was more productive because he spent quality time to up-skill and reskill himself so that with less effort he could produce more results. He sharpened the axe.

The workers of the future go one step ahead. They invest in a new axe to become winners. The losers continue to rely on their outdated, traditional blunt axe; the moderates sharpen their axes; the winners buy a new axe.

Knowledge, Skill and Wisdom

Knowledge means knowing the right thing truthfully. Skill is doing the right thing all the time. Doing right once is luck. Doing it with perfection all the time is skill. Wisdom is one's ability to use knowledge and skills at the appropriate time and situation. Wisdom gives one a holistic outlook and one becomes magnanimous in day-to-day life.

Wisdom is an amalgamation of knowledge, skill, experience, empathy, compassion, values, sound judgement and common sense. The wise make good decisions not only for themselves but for humanity.

The Greeks believed that the wise were those who knew themselves. 'Know Thyself' is considered one of the most ancient Greek aphorisms written in the 20th Century BC in the courtyard of the Temple of Apollo at Delphi.

> Knowledge decides what to say. Skill decides how to say. Wisdom decides how much to say. Goodness decides whether to say it or not.

Wisdom will tell us how we should walk and how far we should walk. It will tell us what to say and how to say it, what to give and how much to give. It will remind us what our responsibilities are and where our influence will end. Wisdom will tell us who we really are.

Knowledge decides what to say. Skill decides how to say. Wisdom decides how much to say. Goodness decides whether to say it or not.

Up-Skill and Reskill for the Future

As we said, digital technology is invading every domain of our life. Professions in engineering, medicine, manufacturing and even sales and service are becoming digital. The experts of today become averages the next day. Up-skilling and reskilling appear in the horizon as the savior for those who want to survive the onslaught of the future of work. Those who up-skill and reskill themselves will be able to harness the latest trends to remain relevant in the workplace.

"How do I up-skill or reskill myself?" "My organization doesn't support in up-skilling." "I have been doing the same work for the last 10 years and have become an expert in that. Why should I up-skill?" These are some common questions that we encounter during trainings.

We are the best to identify the gaps in our performance and skill levels. We know the future is going to be drastically dangerous. Hence it is our responsibility to up-skill or reskill ourselves to become result-givers in future.

The market is full of options to up-skill and reskill. Educational institutions and Massive Open Online Courses (MOOCs) are flooding the market with short and long-term courses to help the learner. As wise professionals, we must choose what is right for us and invest in ourselves to up-skill our capabilities.

If we don't train ourselves, we will lose our jobs and if the organizations don't train their employees, they will lose them to the competition.

New Age Learning to Manage the Future of Work

If the olden days were characterized by rapid urbanization and mechanization of life, the new age is connected by digital technology that is bringing out immense benefits to us. However these benefits are only for those who are willing to learn differently. Many researchers say that 80% of employees require up-skilling immediately. Organizations are worried.

HRDians are working hard to create personalized learning journeys for each employee. They aim to bridge the performance gaps by nurturing talents for the future. They focus on core human skills that will make a difference. Skills like curiosity, critical thinking, innovation, collaboration, synergy, mindfulness and resilience are part of their curriculum.

Leadership is another area of concern. Organizations need leaders who can navigate the waves of change and lead them to the shores of transformation. Leaders with strategic and critical thinking skills can help organizations.

Investing in Subject Matter Experts (SMEs) is another area that many organizations are getting into today. SMEs are assets for the organization as they have strong business acumen and contribute to the return on investment. We need to help the SMEs to reskill and up-skill so that they are trained to become multi-tasking talents to take on different roles in future.

The future is digital and so digital skills are essential for everyone in the organization. I know of organizations that mandate the employees of all levels to complete a common minimum certification program on digital skills including Data Science, AI, IOT, Blockchain and Industry 4.0. These recurring courses can ignite the minds of the employees and prepare them for the future of work.

It is high time that we reinvented the ways of learning. Traditional classrooms with whiteboards, projectors, slides, videos, games, case studies and role plays are out of the window. In future, the learner wants the learning to be democratic, easily accessible at his own space, pace and place through digital and collaborative platforms that are deeply learner-centric.

> People shouldn't become addicted to learning. They must learn, implement the new learning at work and bring return to the organization.

The learners of the future will not have the patience for daylong learning. They are already shifting to micro-learning and bite-sized learning modules. Classrooms have become hybrid. The shorter shelf-life of knowledge and the shorter attention span of the learner are two important criteria driving the learning culture of organizations today.

The belief that 'one size fits all', is outdated. Too much time on screen or in physical classes is causing a lot of fatigue. People shouldn't become addicted to learning. They must learn, implement the new learning at work and bring return to the organization. This is the only task of HRD in future.

There is a tremendous enthusiasm among the HRDians for the new age learning. The positive ripples created by them may transform the way people learn.

The learner is no more a passive recipient. HRD cannot be a monarch. It is not a spectator either. Both have to collaborate and enter into a partnership to continue the momentum created by the ripples of digital transformation.

Organizations that focus on future skills that are both uniquely human and digitally futuristic will survive the disruptions of this revolution. Such organizations will tide over the waves and sustain success.

Democratic Learning

As we said, 'one size does not fit all.' Employees want personal learning plans. They want the freedom to choose what they want to learn so that they can bridge their performance gaps and deliver results. Gamification, recurring certifications, micro-learning modules, incentivized learning programs, social learning platforms and experiential learning opportunities are what the learners of the future are looking for.

When learning is democratic, the organization will be able to retain the top performers, tackle emerging challenges, nurture talents for the future and adapt the organization to manage the changes in the market.

Democratic learning paths are part of the career progression because every individual learns differently. HRD should incorporate these individual learning styles. I have encountered professionals who learn differently. Some learn better under a coach, others in teams, some on the job, some in classrooms while some believe in self-paced learning.

HRD must identify these learning styles and offer its products accordingly. Successful organizations encourage employees to prepare their own learning maps. This way they take ownership of their development.

Democratic learning culture encourages retention and implementation. We know that people remain longer in the organization if we invest in their development. Many employees give lack of training as the major reason for exit. "Train people well enough so that they can leave; treat them well enough so they don't want to", says Richard Branson, founder of Virgin Airlines.

> Democratic learning is the trait of a modern organization.

Democratic learning is a great tool to create employee loyalty and reduce attrition. People leave organizations for various reasons like the lack of learning opportunities. Exit interviews reveal that 70% of attrition is due to the absence of robust career maps and learning programs.

Traits of the Future

The future is unpredictable and volatile. The world is no more static but is in constant flux. New ways of work, workers and workplaces are mushrooming daily. For example, automation has amplified the benefits of technology. We can identify the traits of the future if we look at the evolution of science and technology.

The period of Renaissance that started in the 15th century marked the transformation of the middle ages into a modern world of humanism. This cultural movement brought about a new political climate in the world. The future at that time was unpredictable and those who were unable to align themselves by this humanistic philosophy perished.

During the Age of Reason in the 17th century, human happiness became the focal point of all philosophical and theological discussions. Happiness was to be discovered through rational thinking. Hence there was an urge to separate the divine from the secular realities and reason became the armour to defend human values like liberty, equality, justice and social harmony.

Religious dogmas and religious authorities were debated with a scientific temper. Rationalists like Rene Descartes and Immanuel Kant defined the concepts of enlightenment based on reason. The future appeared uncertain again and those who didn't profess this philosophy were ostracized.

Though mass production and mechanization threatened the 18th century worker, inventions of electricity lighted not only the world but also the human mind. However the workers felt that they were mere machines for production. So they wanted autonomy and a say in what they did. By early 19th century, they began to dream about automation of work though it remained an elusive dream.

Today we speak of autonomous vehicles, IOT and connected life. Cars that were once totally controlled by the drivers, for example, will not require drivers in future. Education will not be enclosed within the physical structures of its campuses. Universities will operate on digital platforms.

The future of many traditional jobs is at risk. The impact of automation is enormous as it reduces not only human efforts and accidents but also performs routine tasks with ease and precision. However it also brings a lot of anxiety for the worker of the future.

Workplaces are radically affected by digitalization. The manufacturer's six day work pattern with eight hours per day is disappearing fast with flexi timings and work from home options. Working hours, duration of work, the place of work and the depth of engagement at work are outdated concepts.

The future wants one to give results not one's time, passion or efforts. Gig economy will replace regular employment; life-long careers will give way to contract based employment; loyalty to the organization will be replaced by loyalty to the customer; product organizations will become service organizations. Moonlighting will be a preferred option. The future will become present.

As hostel boys at Don Bosco institutions, we had the pleasant experience of waking up daily with the sounds of claps from the warden. Though there would be a bell to wake us up, he would walk around the dormitory clapping till all were up. It is still a vivid and nostalgic image in my mind.

Later on, I learnt that this was an age-old practice that originated in Europe. At the time of the industrial revolution, in Britain and in Ireland there was a profession known as the 'knocker-upper.' The expensive alarm clocks were the privilege of the rich.

The destitute, especially on freezing winter mornings, to get up and go to work on time required the help of someone to wake them up on time. So they created a new profession called the 'knocker-upper' whose role was to wake up people so that they would reach the factories on time.

He would go around knocking on the doors or windows of his clients with a long stick to ensure they were awake. There were hundreds of employees who performed this lucrative job until the alarm clock killed it!

The pandemic has caused the advent of the future of work. However learning is still the last item on the bucket list of many. They are too busy with their targets, goals, meetings and profits; training is a distant dream.

Those who take advantage of the changes brought by the future of work will be able to set the sails of their lives along the wind of transformation. They are the new-age learners.

The survivors of this digital massacre will be those who buy a new axe instead of sharpening the existing one.

<table>
<tr><td>3</td><td>

Talents, Pelicans and Footprints

</td></tr>
</table>

The competitiveness and effectiveness of an organization depend on the talents and capabilities of its employees. It depends on how well we fit the right talents in the right place and how well we merge individuals' goals with the organization's goals. If we hire the right talents, develop and manage them, we will be able to handle many of the turnovers, dissatisfactions, low productivity, absenteeism and industrial disputes.

Talents are those qualities and capabilities that are inborn, innate and non-transferable. These are one's natural aptitudes. Literally it means a 'gifted ability'. These may be our abilities in sports, music, arts, and dramas; our intelligence, good health, creative mind and adaptability; our ability to take risks, our discernment skills to foster healthy relationships and our willingness to light a lantern.

Everything bestowed on us by nature is a talent. In fact, we are an ocean of talents. "Every talent is a gift from God. Hence we have the obligation to develop it, not to waste it, for the benefit and progress of humanity", says Pope John Paul II.

Have you heard of the story of the Californian pelicans?

They were the lucky birds who got their food without any work because the fishermen after cleaning the fishes would throw their entrails to them. The pelicans nourished themselves on these entrails. In the meantime, they became fat, lazy and content.

Later on the fishermen discovered ways to commercially use the entrails for better purposes. So they stopped throwing them away. But the pelicans waited and waited for their free food. However no food came. They became weak and thin. They couldn't get food because they had forgotten how to fish. For years they had never used their talents. All of them ultimately starved to death.

Similar tragedies may happen in our lives too. We become inefficient, unproductive and incompetent when we fail to continuously nurture and improve our talents and gifts. The saddest thing is to see a talent going waste. When a talent goes to waste, a person goes to waste.

The real tragedy in life is not being limited to a few talents but the failure to develop and use the talents given to us. As a result, we disappear leaving no footprints on the sands of time. History may forget us but won't forgive us.

> History may forget us but won't forgive us.

Different people have different talents. If you merely look at people and their talents, we will conclude nature is unfair to us as some have more talents than others.

It's ridiculous to think so. Imagine a world with people having the same talents. Suppose this world had only Sachin Tendulkars and no Rajnikanths; what a boring world this would have been!

Variety is beauty. We all don't need the same talents. We need different talents to fulfill the different demands.

The Parable of the Talent

The word 'Talent' comes from the Biblical tradition and is an allusion to the Parable of the Talent narrated by Lord Jesus Christ in the Holy Bible.

A man was on a long journey. Before he set off, he called his servants and entrusted to them his property. The first one was given five talents while the second received two and the third servant got one talent based on each one's ability.

The one who had received five talents went at once and traded and invested them with total commitment and he in the process, made five more talents. The second servant who received two talents did the same and he too made two more talents. However the one who received one talent complained about the partiality of the master and in anger dug a hole in the ground and hid the talent without using it.

After a long time, when the master returned, he called his servants and asked for an account of what he had given them. The first servant who had received five talents came with another five talents and said, "Master, you gave me five talents; here, I have made five talents more.' His master said to him, "Well done, good and faithful servant. You have been faithful over a little; I will set you over much. Enter into the joy of your master."

The second servant who had received two talents came and said, "Master, you gave me two talents; here, I have made two talents more." His master said to him, "Well done, good and faithful servant. You have been faithful over a little; I will set you over much. Enter into the joy of your master."

He asked the third servant what he had done with his talent. He said, "Master, I knew you to be a hard man, reaping where you did not sow and gathering where you scattered no seed, so I was afraid and I went and hid your talent in the ground. Here, you have what is yours."

His master was angry that he had not used his talent at all and said, "You wicked and slothful servant! You knew that I reap where I have not sown and gather where I scattered no seed? Then you ought to have invested my money with the bankers and at my coming I should have received what was my own with interest. So take the talent from him and give it to him who has the ten talents. For to everyone who has will more be given, and he will have an abundance. But from the one who has not, even what he has will be taken away. And cast the worthless servant into the outer darkness where there will be weeping and gnashing of teeth."

Though 'talent' literally meant money, Jesus used it to mean the capabilities, aptitude, skills and gifts bestowed on us and which are to be used for the improvement of ourselves and our society. We have an abundance of talents. It doesn't matter how many talents we possess; what matters is how well we nurture and use them.

These God-given gifts and talents are to be effectively used for the welfare of everyone. If you use your talents, you will receive more talents. If you don't use, you will lose even the little you have.

The challenge for us is to develop our talents and use them well for our own benefit and for the good of others. To become efficient and effective, we need to build on our talents. Many of us are unhappy and unproductive because we fail to build on our talents and fail to choose a career based on our talents. We hide it and complain like the third servant. "Hide not your talents; they for use were made; what's a sundial in the shade", says Benjamin Franklin.

Talents, Skills and Strengths

Talents, skills and strengths are jargons that HR professionals love to use on every platform. For our clarity let us try to differentiate these concepts.

Talent, as we said, is an innate, inborn and non-transferable quality given to us by God. It is our natural aptitude to do something. Examples of talents are our natural ability to sing, dance, paint, tell stories etc. It is our inborn aptitude or interest in mathematics, science, history, sports, arts, music etc.

Skills are learnable and transferable from one person to another. If I don't know how to swim, play volleyball or write an essay, I can learn these skills from trainers and teachers. It is a voluntary act and depends on the learner's receptivity to learn. The teacher helps the learner by formulating steps and processes and by providing the right environment and experience to develop the skills.

> Organizations make the mistake of hiring the best talent and skilling them for something else.

Skill includes three things: knowledge, practice and experience. We don't gain them suddenly but acquire through intense practice, repeated trials and costly errors.

Skills define our future. Talents may help us to stand apart but skills will route our path to success. "The past is in your head, the future is in your hands", says Buddha. Our skills define our destination.

When a person identifies his natural talents and invests in them, it becomes a strength. There are numerous cases wherein people had exceptional talents, but without proper training and support remained as ordinary performers and some even became failures like the third servant in the Parable of Talents. We also have inspiring stories of sportsmen, artists, scientists and noble souls who having identified their talents, patiently invested to develop them to reach outstanding performance in their career.

If a person can sing, it is his talent. But if he is given proper training and handholding, he can turn out to be a world-class singer. Strength is thus built on talent. If we identify our talents, nurture them and skill them up they become our strengths.

Organizations make the mistake of hiring the best talent and skilling them for something else. They create failures at workplaces. We need to work on talents to transform them into strengths. Leaders should give them opportunities to maximize their strengths and not pressures to maximize their weaknesses.

The management at times recruits people and demands 'a fish to fly and a bird to swim.' One can excel only in one's talents. If invested sufficiently these talents can become one's strengths. Skills may help them to perform a role; but excellence comes from strength.

Strength has two characteristics: first, it showcases consistent high performance in a specific area and second, it gives maximum satisfaction to the one who possesses it. We become experts on a particular talent by acquiring sufficient skills, knowledge, practice and aptitude.

We have numerous talents and infinite number of possibilities. We need to discover them. Take time to travel within to recognize those talents buried deep inside. Become aware of the talents we have wasted or thrown away or hidden or those we consider useless. Write down the many things that we can do well. If we make a list of our talents, we will amazingly discover things we never thought we possessed.

Having discovered our talents our next responsibility is to develop them. We must nurture our gifts and make them hundredfold. We have the obligation to multiply our talents by constant practice and use. You alone are responsible for the development of your talents. You alone are responsible for your success.

Everybody is born with a whole set of talents. Talents are gifts because we receive them freely. We can nurture and develop them into skills and strengths. The world is full of competition. Yet the one who has developed his talents and made them into skills and strengths will always find ample opportunities to excel. He will always be in great demand.

The Ruler of 10 Cities

If we continue to read the Parable of the Talent, in the Holy Bible, we see that the first man who received 10 talents is rewarded for his sincere work. He is made the ruler of 10 cities while the second becomes the ruler of 5 cities. This is the result of faithfulness and commitment to one's work. If we are faithful in little things, we will receive rewards, promotions and accolades. On the other hand, if we complain, we deprive ourselves of the compliments and will lose even the little we have.

'Samgo Choyeyo' is a Korean management philosophy used by Korean conglomerates. It means that organizations should hire the best talents and give them ordinary tasks till they show their faithfulness, loyalty and sincerity. Higher responsibilities, promotions and rewards are only for those who multiply their talents faithfully. Rewards should be for the doers not the shirkers!

I had the joy of helping many new joiners who felt obnoxious about this practice. I would spend a considerable amount of time during the induction programs to help them understand the positive power of Samgo Choyeyo. If one is faithful in small tasks, one will also be faithful in big tasks.

You are a Steward of Your Talents

Are we good stewards of our gifts? Stewardship means to take good care of one's resources. We must be faithful, confident and humble in the use of our talents.

Remember, we are stewards not the owners of our talents. We have no right to destroy or bury them. Our duty is to protect, nurture, improve, multiply and use them for the good of all.

As good stewards, we take up the right job to nurture our talents. Choose a job that will require our talents, skills and strengths. Choose the right job where we will be comfortable and competent. Focus on to build a career on strengths and talents. Our talents should help us to become a brand.

> We are stewards not the owners of our talents.

A steward is passionate and committed to his work. We need to become passionate about our talents and develop them daily to get better. Passion for goals will ignite our life and we will begin to use our maximum strength to achieve our goals.

Finally, talents are to be used to make the world better. Some talents we use; some we don't. Like the servants in the Parable of the Talent, we use our talents at times to promote ourselves, sometimes to put down others and sometimes we totally hide them from others. We are given these talents to build up this world not to destroy it.

One way to know whether we are using our talents is to examine ourselves and see if we are really happy in our job. Are we using our talents and strengths? Are we transforming our talents into our core strengths? Have we identified a niche where we can excel and where our competitors may respect our talents? Are we the best person to do a job?

How often does my boss praise and recognize my work? Am I essential in this organization? Am I respected for my contributions and am I valued in the organization? Do people think of my talent as their benchmark? Am I making a difference? Am I happy and content with what I do?

Well, these questions will tell us if we are developing and using our talents or not.

Are we multiplying our talents by hundredfold, fiftyfold or tenfold or have we hidden them somewhere with grudge? Or are we like those Californian pelicans that wait, eat, chat and depart, leaving no footprints on the sands of time?

4 Procrastination: The Weapon of the Imps

Why do some people succeed in life while others don't? It's not because they don't have enough skills, strengths, knowledge, opportunities, passion and potential. They fail because of their attitude to procrastinate.

We put off things at the slightest difficulty. We think we have plenty of time and hope opportunities will come again. As a result, we hope to do it better next time. But alas, opportunities are gone and we end up doing nothing at all. The 'next time' rarely arrives.

Let me narrate a story that I heard a long time ago.

It was the day of convocation in hell. Lucifer was ready to test his little imps as they were leaving their renowned management institute and wanted to test them for the final time. So he asked them what their strategy would be to make human beings commit sin and deploy them in hell.

"I will use a classical approach", said the first imp. "I will tell them there is no God. People will live as if God is not there and they will commit plenty of sins."

"I will use an intellectual strategy", argued the second. "I will tell them there is no hell, so why to worry; do what you want; enjoy; live your life to the full."

"I will use a subtle strategy", answered the third imp. "I will ask them simply, 'why hurry'? There is plenty of time. Do it tomorrow or the day after; why do you want to struggle now?"

Guess who came first in the test. The first rank went to the third imp.

What a silly story! But it has a profound message for all.

How often do we procrastinate and fail in our activities? How often do we regret 'we could have done it earlier?' How miserable and frustrated do we feel today because of the many excellent opportunities we missed in the past? Don't we long to re-live the past devoid of all the mistakes and missed-out opportunities?

Procrastination can sprain our legs and we limp in our profession instead of running to grab it with enthusiasm and passion.

It's one of the major problems we face in life. People who put off things they can do today will never reach anywhere and success always evades them. Look at the innumerable times we put off our plans and dreams.

Look at the numerous times we postponed our to-do lists.

Why do We Procrastinate?

The reasons are many. But the primary reason is our low self-esteem. We have a shallow concept about ourselves and so we are afraid to take the risk of going ahead to achieve our goals. We are comfortable with our present situation. We don't want to change and commit ourselves to a higher goal. We are complacent and complacency is an evil as it lames progress.

Another reason for procrastination is our failure to set goals. The goals should be set along with a timeframe and this will help us to achieve the goals in time.

Define specific, measurable, achievable and realistic goals that can be achieved within a time frame. Next, find out what actions are required to reach that goal. Then walk daily, steadily and strongly towards that goal.

A third reason for procrastination is our instinct to run after too many things simultaneously. In our career, we need to focus on our goals and nothing else. Goals give us meaning, direction and purpose for our lives. When we are not focused, we will get distracted by many things and will always find a reason to postpone. If we have more than one goal, prioritize them according to their importance and urgency.

We procrastinate because we don't have anyone to guide and help us. Identify a mentor to guide you in your professional journey. A mentor can help you to focus your attention and chase your goals instead of chasing something else.

At the end of the day, ask yourself whether you have achieved your target and if not, find out why. This will help you to prevent your tendency to procrastinate. The mentor will help you to walk the right path.

Finally, our irresponsibility and lack of passion are also reasons for procrastination. We make excuses for everything. A responsible and committed person will never postpone things. He knows he is accountable either to somebody or to himself. Making excuses for everything shows us in a deplorable manner. Excuses paralyze us!

'I Have No Time': the Biggest Lie in the World!

According to Tirukkural, the ancient Tamil book of wisdom written in 300 BC, the biggest lie in the world repeated by everyone is 'I have no time'. However if we look at those who are successful, we will find that they do so many things to keep themselves busy and yet they still have some time for new things.

How do they manage their time? How do they gain more time?

Peter Drucker, the management guru, would say that effective executives do not start with their tasks. Rather they start with their time. They make plans based on the available time so that they are able to cut down on unproductive acts that take away their time.

Time is a unique and limiting resource. All other resources, including human resources, are replaceable. Yesterday is gone forever. We can't buy, hire, rent or store it. Though time is freely given, it is priceless! Yesterday is history; tomorrow is mystery; today is the gift and that's why it's called the present!

Time is given free; but it is priceless!

Time is equal to life. If we spend time wisely, we become wise. If you waste your time you become a waste and your life is wasted.

Life, in my view, is a series of events that happen between birth and death. These events can be both pleasant and unpleasant. Some may make us happy while others may give sadness. If we can multiply happy events and learn from the sad events, we will live our lives well.

One of the most common questions I get in my training is 'How to manage time?' So let me share a few practical tools to stop procrastination and enhance our effectiveness as professionals.

1. Prepare a To-Do List

The best way to overcome the spell of the imp is to prepare a good to-do list and faithfully adhere to it. Having a to-do list is one of the best ways to manage time well. It will help us to overcome our tendency to procrastinate.

Do you have a to-do list?

The first thing to be done in the morning as we reach the workplace is to prepare a to-do list for that day. As we complete each task, give a tick mark to that item. Some of the activities may get postponed due to other priorities assigned by the management or due to unforeseen events that may arise on that day. That is ok. Prioritize the tasks again by looking at the to-do list. Focus the attention to more important tasks.

Whenever we start an activity, we must ask ourselves: "Is this something that I need to do today?" As you drive home in the evening review the to-do list in your mind and you will feel more fulfilled and excited because you were able to enjoy a more productive day.

Effectiveness does not mean that one is busy the whole day. It doesn't mean we spend our entire life in the office to show our loyalty to the bosses and the management. Some people stay beyond their work time just because their bosses are around. Next time when the boss is on leave, watch the clock on the wall as you pick up your bags to leave the office. Offices are almost empty after working hours when bosses are on leave.

Once the to-do list is ready, we need to look at it again to prioritize the items based on their importance and urgency. Identify the critical tasks, high-impact tasks, routine tasks and tasks that can be delegated. Critical tasks are those that we have to complete it before the end of the day. High-impact tasks are those key performance indicators that give us maximum results.

Very often in life, we spend a lot of time doing small, routine and unchallenging tasks which give us little visibility in the organization and thus procrastinate the high-impact tasks. Pay attention to this tendency.

2. Prepare a Not-To-Do List

Along with a to-do list, it is also good to have a 'not-to-do list'. This will help us to identify our time wasters. We all waste a lot of time doing unproductive things like surfing the net, uncontrolled usage of social media, too much of TV, gossip and negative talk. The tendency to procrastinate, desire for perfectionism, unproductive meetings, unwanted telephone calls and unsolicited interruptions steal a lot of our time.

Plato says, "An unexamined life is not worth living." We need to identify the purpose of our life and eradicate things that prevent us from reaching this purpose. A 'no-to-do list' is a fantastic weapon in our war against unproductive activities. It can make us disciplined.

"God, it was a busy day", we say so often. But the real question is: "Was I productive or was I busy?" We might have been swamped doing all unproductive and routine tasks. "What was my contribution to my goal?" "How much time did I spend on non-productive tasks?" These are powerful questions to ask ourselves at the end of each day.

3. Say 'No' When Your Heart Wants to Say 'No'

Learn to say 'No'. Some people are overloaded and stressed all the time because they don't know how to say 'no'. As a result, they make more commitments than they can fulfill.

Volunteering is important and noble. However we need to ensure it does not prevent us from doing our primary responsibilities. These are 'nice people' who are afraid to offend others by saying 'no'.

You will become effective if you say 'no' once in a while and help others to do their tasks by themselves instead of taking everything on your shoulders. If you want to lend a helping hand, it's fine, but don't substitute the others and take up their jobs.

Saying 'no' to a boss and peer at times is important. It is a skill that many of us need to develop. Saying 'yes' may help us to look good, but will make you a loser in the long run.

If you find it arduous to say 'no' straightaway to your boss, use strategies like, "I am a little tied up now and so shall we talk about it tomorrow?" If he is wise he will understand your intention and will look for someone else to do his work.

4. Delegate Freely, But Not to the Wolf

Delegation is a beautiful tool for everyone, especially for the leaders. The best way to tackle procrastination and get a long pending work completed is to cut it into smaller tasks and assign them to the right person in the team.

Delegation is one of the crucial traits of a good leader. Many leaders carry the burden of their team members on their shoulders while their team members walk free with no work to do. Don't underestimate your team. They can do many things. Trust them and relax instead of doing their job by yourself. However don't dump unpleasant, uninteresting or unproductive tasks on them.

Delegation means assigning the right work to the right person and giving them the necessary authority and autonomy to perform these tasks. It gives you more time to do bigger things and gives your team motivation and a sense of ownership.

While delegating, make sure to delegate the complete job and jobs that they can do better than you. It gives them a sense of achievement.

However the ultimate responsibility to get the work done will still be yours only.

For delegation to work, you must first of all educate and train the person to whom you are delegating, give the person the power, even the power to make mistakes and also trust that the individual can do an excellent job.

Once upon a time, there lived a shepherd who had many sheep. He would take the sheep to pastures and would also simultaneously do some other tasks like collecting firewood, fruits etc. One day he saw a wolf staring at his sheep. The shepherd was anxious and he tried to chase the wolf away.

Next day again, the wolf came and it was standing nearby harmless watching the sheep. The shepherd seeing that the wolf did no harm, became friendly with the wolf. As the days went by, the wolf even started helping him to take care of the sheep when they moved away from the herd.

The shepherd became so close to the wolf that one day he had to go to the market to sell firewood and fruits that he asked the wolf to take care of his sheep. When he returned, he saw all his lambs killed and eaten by the wicked wolf whom he had trusted.

Don't leave your sheep to a wolf. Delegate your tasks only to people you trust and who will do them on your behalf. Beware of wolfs who will kill your career, reputation and your role in the organization.

It is true as a leader we can't do everything. We need to delegate. Make sure to delegate to the good, able and talented but not to the wolf!

5. Persevere till the Goal

"I trained four years to run 9 seconds and people give up when they don't see results in two months", says Usain Bolt. Difficulties and tough times are not the end of the road. Losing a job, falling in critical illness, failing in exams, being stuck in a traffic jam, losing a dear one and loss in business are not the end of life.

> "The tendency to persevere, to persist, in spite of hindrances, discouragements and impossibilities distinguishes the strong from the weak."
>
> Dr. John Parankimalil

These defeats should not stop us; we have the energy to go ahead with perseverance till we reach our goals. "The tendency to persevere, to persist, in spite of hindrances, discouragements and impossibilities distinguish the strong from the weak", says Dr. John Parankimalil.

Life will shovel all kinds of dirt on us. We need to shake it off, take a step up and walk on with persistence and perseverance. "Great works are performed not by the strong but by those who persevere", says Samuel Johnson, renowned author.

Just as a stonecutter goes on hammering the rock with perseverance and patience without giving up, we too need to continue our efforts. Nothing happens in the first few minutes and at times even for hours. But he keeps on hitting hard and finally his perseverance pays off. With his final blow the rock splits into two. "Genius is 2% inspiration and 98% perspiration", says Thomas Edison.

Many people start well but give up on the way. The achievers, however, persevere till they reach their goals.

6. Live Every Moment

A long time ago, a king in Greece wanted to finish off his general who was becoming a threat to his throne. The king disliked his growing popularity and decided to execute him. One day the king sent a soldier to inform the general that he would be executed the next evening.

When the soldier reached the general's house, he found him celebrating his birthday with his friends. When the crowd heard the sad news, the music stopped abruptly, the celebration ended and people stopped dancing and feasting; for they loved the general much.

"Do not be sad", said the general to his friends. "This is my last party. Please join me and let us celebrate in the best way. Let us complete the feast, for I won't be able to enjoy another one with you my friends", he said. So his friends continued to celebrate with him. His wife was in sorrow; friends were in grief; but the general continued to dance with great fun.

The messenger returned to the king and reported what he had seen at the general's house. "That general is out of his mind. He is not afraid of you or death. When I informed him about his execution he seemed to be happier and began to celebrate even more", reported the soldier.

The king was surprised at the behaviour of the general. He decided to visit his house to see what was going on there. He found the general happily drinking and dancing with his friends.

"Are you not sad and frightened that I am going to kill you?" asked the king.

"I know death awaits everyone", replied the general. "We don't know when it will arrive. Hence we live in its fear. Now that you were kind enough to tell me about my death, I am happy to know how much time I have left to celebrate my life. Life is short now for me. However I must live every moment. I have no time to postpone or procrastinate. Thank you for defining my life and for making it definite", he told the king.

The king was so pleased with the attitude of the general that he not only spared his life but also became his disciple. He taught the king how to live every moment. Tomorrow is unsure for everyone. Today is the gift we have. Shall we live our lives king's size?

7. Love Time

Do you love time? Or do you hate time? Those who love time, live lovely lives! Those who hate time live miserable and may even end their lives. The best way to be happy is to fall in love with time!

When you love time, you love everyone around you and you won't have time to hate anyone. I know that not everyone will like me or accept me. But that's ok. If we love time we will choose the company of those who make us confident. We make mistakes. So too everyone. But mistakes make us greater.

The problem with us is that we look for a place to be happy; we look for friends who make us happy; we seek status, wealth and power to be happy. However love, happiness and contentment are not found in places or in people. We experience them in time. We need to create such moments by loving the time at our disposal. Ultimately if we love time, we love our life!

The one who loves time lives in the present. He lives a life of gratitude and grace. In the Holy Bible, St. Paul, in his letter to the Colossians says, "Let your conversation be always full of grace, seasoned with salt, so that you may know how to answer everyone." Loving time thus means to live in grace in the present.

> "Let your conversation be always full of grace, seasoned with salt, so that you may know how to answer everyone."
> St. Paul

As we said, time is one of the most critical and irreplaceable resources at our disposal. Do we then, have a choice to hate it? Shall we cherish it instead of just winding it? Shall we invest time in doing things that make us happy?

Purpose, Prioritization and Progress

If we know the purpose of every activity, learn how to prioritize our 'to-do lists' and delegate them to progress, then we will be able to liberate ourselves from the slavery of procrastination.

"What is the purpose of this activity? Why am I doing what I am doing?" These are questions that we must ask at the start of every task. Eliyahu M Goldratt, the author of the best seller 'Goal' says, "Productivity is the act of taking us closer to our goals. Every action that does not bring us closer to our goals is an unproductive act."

Am I getting closer to my goals or am I moving away from them? Am I just running faster or am I running faster in the right direction? We need to do things for the right reason and for the right purpose. Do we have a purpose in life? Do we prioritize the goals? Are we making progress? These are powerful questions to reflect on as we progress in life.

'A stitch in time saves nine', says the proverb. It reminds us to do things at the right time by prioritizing. If we fail, tasks begin to pile up and become urgent.

Brian Tracy, author and leadership coach in his book 'Eat That Frog' says that successful people know and practise the art of prioritization. They focus on the important things and do them without procrastination.

Hyrum W Smith, missionary, pastor and founder of Franklin Quest Company, formulated the Time Management Matrix that has helped millions of people from across the globe to live a more meaningful and purposeful life. With this powerful tool, one can learn to plan, prioritize, delegate and delete tasks. It will help one to identify and eliminate time wasters. It allows one to gain more time and progress in life.

More than 50% of millennials today value time more than money. Taking away their personal time is a crime. The Gen X demonstrates their loyalty by remaining beyond the work timings. They glamorize working beyond work hours and give higher scores at appraisals to those who stay longer hours at work. The millennial, on the other hand, looks at it as exploitation by the seniors. Many organizations are getting derailed because of the conflicts between the generations.

We need to make time more meaningful by enriching the lives of those around us. We need to add value to their time. We need to help them to live a life of purpose.

The Five D's of Success

The five D's of success are: Delay, Delete, Diminish, Design and Delegate. I use this technique in my life and share it with my participants.

There are trivial things that don't require urgency. They can be delayed or ignored. There are areas that don't require micromanagement. There are decisions that are not crucial or critical. We may delay them.

There are things that are neither urgent nor important. These are things that can be deleted totally or diminished at times. For example, watching TV is not urgent or important. Many of us don't like to delete it totally but would love to diminish it to gain more productive time.

Once we prepare a 'to-do list' we will be able to identify many tasks that don't require our attention. These are jobs that can be performed much better by others. They can be delegated.

Time Management Matrix

	Urgent	Not Urgent
Important	Do	Decide
Not Important	Delegate	Delete

There are tasks that we postpone because either we don't like them or because they are too huge. Instead, we should design them again and make them into smaller chunks for us to chew more comfortably.

"Determining how much time is required for a task and evaluating how much time we currently spend for that task will help us save a lot of time," says Dr. Benny Basil, educator and economist from Guwahati. He is a meticulous planner, an effective delegator and a highly successful professional. If we list down areas where we spend too much time and identify areas that require our time and attention, we will be able to work more effectively.

Do You Have Some Time?

I have failed to reach my goals and destination despite having the best resources and opportunities. I realized it was because I neglected the important and went after the safest and the easiest. I was happy to remain busy though not productive.

Studies show that 85% of our happiness comes from happy relationships with people close to us. But we live unhappy because we have no time for them. How much time do we spend with people we love? Very little!

Many people spend most of their precious time on negative talk. Shall we invest our time wisely to talk positive about others? Spending time on positive things is the key to happiness.

We have been under the influence of the smartest imp and procrastinated on important tasks. We have failed to give our time to those who love us. In the blind pursuit of our goals, we lost many friends and well-wishers and injured many relationships.

We gained skills but lost many opportunities to become wise and good. Beware of the little imp going around influencing us to procrastinate. Let us defeat him before he defeats us.

5 Less of Me and More of We

The most remarkable trait of humanity is that humans can't exist alone. One of my favourite hymns is "No man can live as an island, journeying through life alone." We have never been individually self-sufficient or fully independent. We have progressed from individual existence to collective existence. We have migrated from herd living to community living, from individual work to collaborative work and from individual thinking to team thinking.

The industrial revolution modernized the world and gave birth to a democratic type of functioning in governments and organizations. This produced pretty good results as well. People today are convinced that teamwork and collaboration are essential to success.

> "No man can live as an island, journeying through life alone."
>
> **From a Hymn**

Human life is complex just as the human mind is complex. Mutual help and support are essential to perform these complex tasks. Creativity and success come when we work together. In a team, we can efficiently use the resources, ensuring that there is less wastage of time and resources. This is based on our faith that none of us is as smart and bright as all of us.

In a team, we inspire one another to exhibit high commitment. Each member thus contributes his or her maximum and honestly praises the contributions of others. We treat everyone as important whether big or small. Each individual is unique, important and essential. Each has a role to play in fulfilling its mission.

The team members influence and help one another to accomplish team goals. The members interact with one another often and have an immense desire to belong to the team. They communicate among themselves often and minimize the unresolved conflicts and power struggles through dialogues and transparent conversations.

> "Alone we can do so little; together we can do so much."
>
> Helen Keller

They cooperate and collaborate to achieve the team and the individual goals so that everyone in the team wins. Helen Keller reminds us that "alone we can do so little; together we can do so much". For this to happen, all must think win-win. It is an attitude that says 'all of us can win'. This thinking is the foundation of teamwork.

The success of others shouldn't threaten us. Instead, celebrate their victories if you wish to be successful. It is difficult but this helps us, ordinary people, to achieve extraordinary results.

Do we believe in teamwork? Rarely! Though we appreciate the manifold benefits of collaboration, we prefer to work in silos. This is because teamwork is not easy work. It is more comfortable to go solo.

If we choose to work in a team, we must listen to the ideas of others, debate on their ideas, respect their ideas, persuade them to have better ideas, encourage them to share their problems, help them in their lives and encourage everyone to participate in the team's activities. At times we may have to give up our views too. Too many roles to perform; too many obstacles to manage; but the results are manifold.

An effective team is characterized by well-defined roles for the members, concrete goals and open and direct communication In addition, a team will always be led by a leader.

Stages of Team Development

The model proposed by Bruce Tuckman in 1965 is still helpful to recognize the various stages of team development. Every team and every relationship, including marriages, go through these stages of development.

Tuckman calls the first stage 'Forming'. At this stage, the team comes together and gets oriented with one another. A new employee or a new boss in a team, a newly married couple or even a set of new friends, everyone goes through this experience. The first experience at this stage is good, pleasant and exciting.

However, the pleasant feeling ends very soon. They move into the second stage called 'Storming'. Conflicts and disagreements characterize this stage. Here, the team members try to clarify their individual roles and begin to challenge the way the team functions. In marriage, the honeymoon abruptly ends with the storming stage. People who loved each other much and saw stars in the eyes of the other, suddenly begin to keep a distance and start to see the faults in the other.

Fortunately, they move on to the third stage called the 'Norming' stage. At this stage, the team members agree on the roles of each person. They decide to appreciate the contributions of others and begin to accept the other as they are. In a marriage, for example, if the couple doesn't  reach this stage, it will collapse and may end up in divorce. Likewise, if a new employee does not reach this stage he will soon quit the company.

The fourth stage is called the Performing stage. Here the team decides to perform the roles for which the team was formed. They face problems together, take responsibility for solutions and share the credit. The new couple, for example, is able to align their goals and come to an agreement for the benefit of the family. They decide to uphold the sacredness of the commitment they have made to each other.

The final stage is called 'Adjourning'. Since the team has reached the goal for which the team was formed, it decides to disband itself. Every team is formed with a specific objective in mind. Once the objectives are achieved the team has to dismantle itself or set new goals to achieve.

All these happen within a frontier called 'less of me and more of we.'

Together We Stand, Alone We Fall

The allegory of the Red Wood Trees has always fascinated me. The Red Wood trees are seen in Amazon forests and live up to even 2000 years. They are some of the tallest trees in the world. They stay tall and strong, despite the weather, storms and floods.

How come? They create synergy. Botanists say that the secret to this long life is that their roots are interlinked and interrelated. If one tree decides to stand alone, it will fall. Wisely said, "Together we stand, alone we fall."

The winter was severe and many animals had already perished in the cold. The wise porcupines realizing the gravity of the situation, decided to stay together. So they covered and protected themselves from the extreme cold by staying close to each other. But the quills of each one wounded and pained the closest neighbour though they got warmth from each other. This irritated them. They began to quarrel among themselves. Finally they decided to stay away from each other.

Now they were free of wounds and pains caused by the quills of their neighbour but were under the pangs of severe cold. They began to die one by one.

It was time to make a choice again: either to stay close and experience the quills or die. They decided to stay together with their minor wounds to survive the major challenge.

The warmth, the other gives is life-giving not only for the porcupines, but even us. Living together is a challenge; it may cause injuries, pain and discomfort but it's the only way to survive today.

> Living together is a challenge; it may cause injuries, pain and discomfort but it's the only way to survive today.

The Boat Racers of Kerala

Onam is the harvest festival of Kerala, the southern state of India, popularly known as 'God's Own Country' because of its lush green hills, enchanting backwaters, serene and healthy atmosphere and friendly people. People from across the globe travel to the backwaters during the festival to watch the world-famous boat race locally called the 'vallam kali'.

People dress up for the occasion in traditional attire, compete as a team forgetting all differences, take pride in decorating their boats and boost their sense of belonging to the team. 'Vallam kali' and the accompanying 'vanchi pattu', the paddlers song, have become the brand icons of every Keralite.

The annual sport originated in the 13th century as part of a military necessity among the warring local feudal kings. They built long boats to carry arms and ammunition to the battalions that were engaged in war. The weaponry had to reach in large quantity at the quickest time. After the war, the race continued as part of military training and today the sport is organized as a symbol of unity.

The boat is 138 meters long. The head part is raised to 20 feet high and the tail end looks like the tail of a snake. The boat can carry 100 paddlers, a singer and a leader. The leader stands at the centre blowing a trumpet. The singer sings the 'vanchi paattu' to create the right rhythm and music to the sound of the trumpet. The paddlers paddle in unison according to the rhythm and focused on the goal. Each paddler plays his part to perfection. If one misses the rhythm the whole race collapses.

They collaborate to create the perfect synergy. Once on the boat, all are equal though each plays a different role. The paddlers, the leader, the singer, the carpenters, the boat makers and the club members are not professionals but ordinary people who have decided to come together to win. Ordinary men and women who believe in teamwork will deliver extraordinary performance.

The Roles in a Team

As we said, teams consist of people who perform different roles. These roles are essential for any team as it goes through the various stages of development.

1. The Leaders

They have a vision and a goal to achieve. They are sure and steady, stick to a job until it is done. Nothing else matters to them. They want the goals of the team to be achieved. They bring courage and conviction when people begin to doubt and face trouble.

The leaders push, pull, inspire, motivate and take everyone to the team's goal. They make the team accountable. No team can exist without a leader.

2. The Followers

These are the sheep following the shepherd and they are very supportive of leaders. They are ready to try out anything that the leader tells them. They exist because of the leader and are willing to go to any extreme to make the leader and the team succeed.

They wait for the leader's command and they act on it with their whole heart. They stand by the leader, keep him at the centre and protect him like a royal army.

3. The Innovators

The innovators are the creative and idea people. They offer the sparks. They come up with some innovative ideas when the team is lost and seems to reach nowhere.

They can also be the sources of conflict as they stick on to their ideas and push their views on others. They may be stubborn but are integral part of every team.

4. The Solvers

They love problems and can solve them at an amazing speed. When everyone is breaking heads to discover solutions, here comes the messiah with an out-of-the-box solution often based on his experience or gut feelings.

A leader needs such talents in his team as they support him when faced with a crisis. The problem with these people is that since they love problems, if there are no issues in the team, they will induce some problems.

5. The Synergisers

They provide unity and support and are exceptionally great at bringing harmony and calmness when there are storms in the team. When faced with conflicts, ego and personal clashes, these are the messiahs of hope, friendship and trust. The values of collaboration, relationship and trust are close to their heart.

6. The Humorists

These are fun-loving people and bring cheer and joy when everybody gets lost or when times are tough. When the team faces stress and pressure, is overwhelmed by targets and life becomes rough and tough, these people step in with humour to ease the situation and assure everyone that the situation will be better soon.

They give hope. They assure the team that there is a ray of hope beyond the clouds. They love fun. They energize the teams. They paint a better future for all.

Collaboration: the Oldest Skill

Some of the oldest skills humans learned to survive the onslaught of natural calamities, wild animals and enemies were communication, collaboration and cooperation. They also learnt coordination and political skills to manoeuvre and manipulate their positions in society.

Collaboration is a core value not only in family, society or in governance but also in many corporates. It rests on trust and on

> Some of the oldest skills humans learned to survive the onslaught of natural calamities, wild animals and enemies were communication, collaboration and cooperation.

the spirit of sharing. It ensures prosperity for everyone not just for the leaders. In fact collaboration ensures the collective effort of everyone to achieve the team goal. It is surprising that in this collaborative effort, there are no leaders but only influencers who influence each other to cooperate with whole heart and soul.

A team will always have a leader who will guide the team to achieve the goals. Collaboration is democratic while teamwork by nature is autocratic. A leader transforms teamwork into collaborative work.

In today's turbulent world, working together is unpredictable and highly challenging. Collaboration thus demands empathy and understanding and calls for a cohesive and communitarian culture rooted in trust and loyalty.

We need to encourage and reinforce togetherness by sowing the seeds of relationships, nurturing them and learning the art of dialoguing and connecting with people. To succeed, everyone needs to hone and sharpen the skills of collaboration.

Trust: the Foundation of Teamwork

The fundamental element in teamwork is trust. This is the foundation on which the team stands. However, we all suffer from certain amnesia about what others have done to us and we begin to look at them with suspicion.

Trust gets its expression through cooperation and taking responsibility for the individual's and team's work. Trust nourishes when we listen to people actively and accept that the team is more important than our egos.

The perfect example of collaboration and teamwork is the circus. In a circus, if each artist wants to outshine the other and perform a one-person show, there cannot be a circus show. Unlike in films, there is no 'superstar' in a circus. It has only 'superstars'!

In the same way, the pit-stop of Formula One is another perfect example of synergy and trust. In a pit-stop there are 23 people working in perfect harmony, sharing ideas, information and experience to create the ideal synergy to make the team win. The time given for a pit-stop's work is just 3 seconds! Imagine the amount of synergy, trust and sharing that happens in 3 seconds among these 23 people!

Each one has a different role to perform. Each one has to do that role perfectly and also at the same time should know how the others are progressing in their work.

They work in perfect harmony. Each one in the team is so important that he can make or break the team entirely. If we have the same spirit of trust and collaboration, all of us can be winners!

Brian Cavanaugh, in his book 'The Sower's Seed of Encouragement' narrates an interesting story on teamwork. A famous organist who was known for taking credit and accolades for himself was performing a concert in front of a huge audience one day using an antique organ. The organ bellows were hand-pumped by a servant boy, who was part of his team, from behind a curtain. The boy was unseen by the audience.

The musician was in his full glory and pride as usual. The audience appreciated the musician with a standing ovation as the organizers announced a break. As the musician was walking out of the stage he heard the boy say, "We played well, didn't we sir?"

The organist turned to the boy with complete sarcasm and said, "What do you mean 'we'? It's me who played the music."

After the interval, the audience reassembled to listen to the musician's magic. But this time nothing happened. No music, not a sound was heard. Then the organist heard the boy's voice again from behind the curtain, "Sir, now do you know what 'we' means?"

If you want your team to succeed, if you wish to succeed in life, live this philosophy: 'less of me and more of we.'

6   To San Salvador or To India?

Historians say that Christopher Columbus, the Italian explorer, landed in San Salvador instead of India, as he didn't have a decent map to navigate and steer the direction of his voyage. Columbus began his voyage on Santa Maria on 3rd August 1492 and reached the Americas on 12th October the same year. His intention was to reach Asia and he always thought that the place he landed was in Asia which he called 'earthly paradise.'

He named the land as San Salvador which is today part of Bahamas and called its inhabitants 'Indios' a Spanish word that means 'Indians'.

Columbus started his voyage well. Only to reach the wrong destination!

Like Columbus, we too at times fail in life not through a lack of good intentions, talents or resources but through a lack of purpose and direction.

In our life-journey our goals give us direction. The problem is that many of us do not have any goals and get marooned.

Years ago, while facilitating a career guidance program for a group of University students in Guwahati, I was shocked to discover that 80% of my participants didn't have any goals. They were going through some kind of postgraduate programs without having any idea as to what they really wanted in life. When I asked them what they wanted in life, most had no clues and some replied, "Get married and settle in life." My further study revealed that 95% of adults too don't have any goals either!

> Goals give us meaning and direction to our lives.

It is important to realize that setting goals is the first step to successful and happy life. It gives us meaning and direction in life. Our goals tell us where we are going and why we are going there. They can motivate us, boost our self-confidence and can make us winners. Goals inspire us and make our lives worthwhile. They keep us alive! They inspire us to move on!

People with a goal have an added reason to prolong their life even when faced with a critical illness. My uncle was on his deathbed. He was dying, yet we could feel that something in him motivated him to carry on. Whenever he was awake, he would ask for his elder daughter who was in the northern part of India. He waited for her to arrive.

When she reached, they spoke to each other, she held his hand and in an hour he left us. The goal of seeing his daughter for the last time kept him alive.

Why to Have Goals?

Do we want to succeed in life? Do we want to live a life of happiness and contentment? If our answer is 'yes', we must set our goals high. Successful people set goals. Higher the goals, greater is the success! Clear and specific goals are the foundation of their success. "If you don't stand for something you will fall for anything," says a Chinese proverb.

We all need to have goals to become successful and happy. Or else we will wander around the nectar of happiness and will never have the opportunity to taste its sweetness.

People with no goals are condemned to be slaves of those with goals. Leaders know their goals. They lead their followers to achieve their goals. Goals give us direction, purpose for our existence and make our lives thrilling. A life without goals is worthless!

We fail to set goals due to fear of failure, lack of ambition, fear of rejection, low self-esteem, due to our habit of procrastination and our inability to understand the importance of setting goals.

Our goal is the destination where we want to be in future. Hence it should determine our planning, personal strategy and allocation of resources.

Transform Dreams to Goals

We are dreamers and we dream a lot. But dreams are not goals. Dreams become real when they are supported by what I call as the five D's of success. They are: direction, dedication, determination, discipline and deadliness. "Passionately plant your dreams in your mind, nurture them with care and you will achieve them", says Dhanya Shanmugam, NLP trainer and Chief Learning Officer at a prominent asset management company in Chennai.

Dreams are good. However no one became great just by dreaming. We must convert our dreams into goals by taking specific and measurable actions.

As a trainer, I had the fortune to help hundreds of my participants to achieve their goals. Every now and then, I come across my participants, who attended the training more than a decade ago. They would share with me stories about the goals they had set. Some have built houses, bought cars, taken the family for a foreign trip, completed a post-graduation, written a book, got a promotion or started a business. These were goals set by them. It is comforting to hear such happy stories.

Their dreams became a reality because they moved from the 'dream world' to a 'goal world'. "Dreams are not those that you see while sleeping. They are something that let you not sleep", says Dr. APJ Abdul Kalam.

Are Our Goals Our Own?

Our goals should be our own. This is the first step to achieve the goals. Never shirk the responsibility for what we choose. Instead, take responsibility for life and determine the right goals based on what we have. Choosing a career, for example, because of the suggestions of others often will end up in unhappiness, depression and disasters.

Doing something because someone asked us will not keep us happy for long. We must be convinced of its need and usefulness and do it because we believe this is our life's mission. Our goals must be our own.

The problem is that we have too many goals. Some are our own while some are thrust on us. As a result, we are confused, frustrated and are unable to achieve any of them. We hop from one goal to another looking for the best, the biggest, the most recent and the most

challenging. We also fail to give our entire self to any of these goals because they are not our own.

"My child does not listen to what I say." "My son has no goals." "I don't know what my daughter's future will be." I hear these concerns from parents whenever I facilitate programs for them. Parents thrust their goals on their children. What they couldn't achieve in life, they hope to achieve through their children. They treat them as tools to get what they desired or missed in life.

My wife told me a tragic story about one of her colleagues. As a student he wanted to become a doctor. However he got disqualified in the entrance exam and so had to give up his dream. He became a professor instead. Later on, he decided to make both his sons doctors. The elder son responded positively to his father's goal and became a successful doctor.

When it came to the younger son, he opposed the idea as he wanted to have a career in visual media. Finally, after a lot of arguments and threatening, the boy sacrificed his dream for the sake of his dad. He failed miserably in the first year. One day, after a heated argument between the father and the son, the boy gave up his life.

Our media is full of such tragic stories. When we push our dreams and goals on others, remember we are killing their dreams and at times their lives. If we want them to succeed, their goals should be their own.

"To make the goals our own, the first thing to be done is to know what we want, what we crave for and what we dream of", says Anusha Sriramana, Director, Skillzen Learning. At the outset, we must find out where we are heading, whether we have the resources to reach that destination and whether we are passionately committed to reach that target. For this, we must examine our interests, find out what we are good at and then based on our talents and strengths, we must set our goals.

In other words, we need to begin this journey by understanding who we are, what we have and where our passion is. This is the foundation on which we set our goals.

When we have our own goals we tell our subconscious mind that we are serious about these goals. Then our minds will tell us what we need to do and what we need to give up to achieve our goals.

Are Our Goals SMART?

Having known ourselves the next step in successful living is to set goals that are SMART: specific, measurable, achievable, realistic and time-bound. We should also develop a strategy to achieve these SMART goals.

Smart people like you should have smart goals.

A goal will become specific if it is written down on paper. What do you want in life? Write it down today. What do you want to become? Write it down today. Keeping goals only in mind is as good as not setting them. If you want to achieve any goal, it must be written down in black and white.

Our goals should be measurable for we know we can accomplish only what we can measure. "I want to become an excellent manager." "I want to become a good spouse and an affectionate mother." "I plan to be a benevolent father and a faithful son." However, these are not measurable goals. Excellence, goodness, greatness etc. are adjectives that are not measurable. One can achieve only those things that one can quantify and measure.

The goals that you set should be achievable. A goal like going to the moon is an unachievable goal for most of us. Or saving 25 lakhs per annum when one's salary is 10 lakhs per annum is an unachievable goal. Also we need to set our goals based on the resources we have and at the same time they must be challenging and involve some risk.

Many people set unrealistic goals. If you want to achieve your goals they should be realistic. Let us imagine that a tortoise after reading an inspiring research on SMART goals or having completed a training on smart goals sets for himself a goal like this: 'From today, I will be a rabbit.' Can a tortoise ever become a rabbit? Of course not!

It's an unrealistic goal. Even if the tortoise makes the best efforts, it will never become a rabbit. It can only become a better tortoise. This is a realistic goal.

Finally, the goals should be time-bound. Achieve the goals in the given time. Whatever goals the players shoot after the final whistle in a football match will not make them winners. They need to score in the given time while the game is on.

> A smart goal is like a propellant, it can push us into action.

If our goals are not smart we are bound to fail. If they are smart, we are sure to succeed in our struggles because these are goals that we set on the basis of our strengths and opportunities. We believe that we are capable of achieving them and we use every ounce of our energy to achieve them. These goals are high but achievable.

Smart goals push us to take action. A plan in mind is good. But that is futile unless it is put into action. We need to convert this plan into a smart goal if we are serious about achieving it. "A smart goal is like a propellant; it can push people into action", says Prof. Raja Rajan, faculty of HR, XIME Chennai.

Goals can Inspire

Our goals must inspire us and push us with passion and enthusiasm even in the midst of difficulties so that we go forward with total commitment till we achieve them.

If we have inspiring goals, we won't wait for praises. We will feel good chasing such worthy goals because they are our own goals. These are goals we really want, not merely feel good about. If they inspire and excite us, we will achieve them.

Big and audacious goals can inspire anyone. Small goals are like hobbies. When you set goals, make sure they are significant, challenging and inspiring. They will push you to wake up in the morning with positive energy. They will make you feel proud of your accomplishments. They will inspire you to sleep less and work more.

Sometimes our goals threaten us. They are more like a risk than a goal. Though risks are essential in life, risks that are too big and beyond our reach are folly. Goals, on the other hand, inspire, energize and motivate us to surpass our limits to surprise ourselves.

Fuel Goals with Passion

Many of us set goals and forget about them. If you want the dreams to become real, you must have total commitment, passion and enthusiasm. We should be like a fish that feels so uncomfortable out of the water if we don't achieve our goals. It doesn't mean that we reach every one of our goals. But we do our part and even if we fail in some goals we continue the struggle for the struggle itself gives us meaning and joy.

We can accomplish what seems impossible and beyond our wildest dreams if we have this unquenchable desire and passion to win. Passion for goals pushes us to success. Passion is like the fuel that ignites our efforts to reach the goals.

> We are responsible for our success and failure, our present and future. We are solely responsible for where we are today and where we will be tomorrow.

Passion helps us to focus our thoughts on goals. Thoughts become things. Our goals must dominate our thoughts. We must think of them at every moment.

Never forget the reason why we are here and why we are doing a particular activity. Make a habit of thinking about the goals every day. What we think of constantly will become part of us.

Imagine that we will succeed in our goals. Visualize success every day and we will be successful. Ask ourselves in the morning as we set out for the day: "What can I do today to achieve my goals?" In the evening, as we retire to rest, ask again: "What have I done today to achieve my goals?" This will push us to make things happen.

Seek the Support

We need to get the support of others: our parents, spouse, mentors, teachers, leaders and friends if we want to reach our goals. Share with them your dreams and ask for advice and guidance. They will help you to set achievable goals.

If we set goals that are too high we become frustrated, hopeless and even suicidal. We need immense guidance to set smart goals.

Success comes when we take responsibility for our goals. Others can help us but we alone are responsible for its achievement. We are responsible for our success and failure, our present and future. We are solely responsible for where we are today and where we will be tomorrow. However the good people around us can speed up this process.

Make Impossible Possible

The difference between impossible and possible is determination. How determined are we when it comes to our goals?

One day Buddha asked his disciple to bring the most robust material in the world. He brought a hard rock. Buddha asked him, "What is stronger than the rock?" The disciple thought about it and said, "What is stronger than the rock is the iron because it can break the rock."

"What is stronger than iron?" asked Buddha. "Fire is stronger than iron", replied the disciple, "Because it can melt iron." "What is stronger than fire?" asked Buddha. "Water is stronger than fire" replied the disciple. "What is stronger than water?" "Wind is stronger than water as it can change its direction", said the disciple. "What is stronger than the wind?"

The disciple had no more answers. Buddha smiled gently and said, "Stronger than all these is the determination of human beings."

A person with fierce determination will have everything under his control. Disappointments, disapprovals and discouragements suffocate us. Determination defeats all these and makes things possible. How determined are we to make the impossible possible?

Celebrate the Journey not just the Success

Finally, to reach where we set out, we need a compass called 'fun.' We must set short-term and long-term goals.

When we achieve short-term goals we must take time to congratulate ourselves and celebrate these successes. It will give us more self-confidence and will fill us with passion and dedication to go after the bigger goals. Invite others to join this fun journey and seek humbly for their help and support.

Fun gives one the positive energy to go ahead to become boisterous. Studies have shown that if we enjoy what we do, we are more likely to succeed. For example, I began to dislike Maths as a student because I didn't like my teacher. Soon I found Maths to be the toughest subject. I began to score higher when I had another teacher who taught me to learn the subject with fun. The fun became so addictive that I went on to become a Maths teacher!

Sometimes we are too worried about the results that we fail to enjoy the process. Some of us wait for the final result to celebrate. This wait might take us nowhere. If we celebrate the small successes, we might soon be in the progress of reaching our big goal. We must enjoy the journey. Of course, we need to dream about our destination. But we shouldn't wait to get there to celebrate.

Celebrate the journey and the progress. Focusing too much on the destination may scare and tear us. If we only stare at the top of the mountain, we continue to remain at the valley. We must take baby steps, tread them smartly and enjoy each step. Fun is the medicine when negative thoughts come to ruin our spirits.

When was the last time you celebrated a victory with your family and colleagues? When was the last time you posted your adventures and achievements on social media? What prevents you from praising yourself? Why are you shy of appreciating yourself? Go out and speak about your successes, both small and big.

Celebrate more to achieve more in life. Small successes are important; celebrate them and it will give you the enthusiasm to move towards the next victory. Celebrate your journey to your goal. Repeated successes will offer you more self-esteem and self-confidence to become more productive and happy.

Expect failures as well. However, don't be threatened by them. Rather learn from them and walk ahead steadily and firmly to your goals.

Conflict between Personal and Organizational Goals

Every organization has a set of goals. Every organization is made up of people who also have their own personal goals. It is important that we as employees learn the skills to align these two. While working hard to achieve organizational goals, we must also ensure that we achieve our personal goals.

Most of the time, as employees, we will be able to reach our goals only by helping our organization to reach its goals. The growth of the company is proportional to our growth. People, at times, ask me what they should do when they face a conflict between their personal and organizational goals.

> The growth of the company is proportional to our growth.

Goal alignment is vital for all. Our goals should be aligned with our organization's goals. As employees, we must clarify our goals and compare our goals with the organization's goals to identify if there is any mismatch. The more we can make this alignment, the more successful we will be.

When we reach a stage of alignment, what we do to achieve the organization's goals will contribute to achieve our own goals. If we notice that the goals of the organization are not in line with our personal goals, as employees, we have no option but to perform these obligations to achieve organizational goals. This is part of our accountability and responsibility.

Conflict happens when we realize that our goals are incompatible with those of the organization. I tell my participants that when they face this type of crisis, they have two options: either follow the goals and quit the organization or follow the organization and give up their goals. It's a choice one must make based on one's priorities and commitments in life.

Set your goals high. If you don't reach them, it's ok; you will at least put on muscles climbing toward them. If we have a goal, we will not wait for opportunities but make everything into an opportunity to achieve that goal. Goals that command our thoughts, liberate our energy and inspire our hopes will fill us with fulfilment.

If we don't know where we want to go, then we will land like Columbus where we never desired to reach.

I recently read that 80% of the wealth of this world is in the hands of 20% of people. And who are this 20%? They are the rich. They are the ones with goals. The irony is that the 80% plough hard day and night to make the 20% richer! They are the 'goalless' and are condemned to be slaves of those with goals.

Live with smart goals; don't be another Columbus!

7

The Taming of a Wild Bull

Millions of people suffer from a deadly disease called glossophobia. This is one of the biggest fears in human life second only to the fear of death. In my interactions with people, I have rarely found anyone who does not become panicky if he needs to be on stage to deliver a speech.

One of the traits of successful professionals is that they possess the power to influence their listeners through fearless speeches. Fear not only handicaps one's performance but also derails one's career.

Do you experience nervousness, stuttering, nausea, dizziness, tremor or indigestion while on stage? Do your hands shiver, voices tremble, stumble for words, sweat profusely, mouths become dry and minds become blank when on stage?

If yes, then it's a natural sign of being human. All humans fear being on stage.

> "I am a man who is afraid. All the wise men I know are afraid."
> Dr. Harold Urey

"I am a man who is afraid. All the wise men I know are afraid", says Dr. Harold Urey, Nobel Peace Prize winner and one of the greatest physicists whose work led to the invention of the atomic bomb. So be glad if you are afraid of the stage. You are in the league of the wise!

However those who defeat glossophobia through passion and practice will love being on stage. They have mastered the art of taming the wild bull!

Some physicians consider stage fear as an illness. It is a curable disease anyway. They believe it is a social anxiety disorder caused due to a fear of rejection, an unhealthy evaluation by others, a fear of failure or an imminent experience of embarrassment. Just as a cat that fell into hot water once is always afraid of water, we are also scared of public speaking because of past unpleasant experiences.

The Jallikattu inside Us

Pongal, the harvest festival of Tamil Nadu in South India, brings people a lot of joy, fun and happiness. Jallikattu, originated in 400 BC, is part of every Pongal celebration. It is a sport that demonstrates bravery and skill.

During the festival, ferocious, well-bred and gigantic bulls are released among the crowd of contestants. The sight of the bulls sends trepidation and fear to the audience. The contestants have to tame the wild bulls by grabbing the large hump on the top of the bull. They need to hold on to the hump, pull the chasing bull to a dead stop and remove the flag from its horn to be declared a winner.

It's a dangerous sport. Many get severely wounded and a few even get killed. However in their resolve to defeat fear and showcase bravery, they immerse themselves into the battlefield to tame the wild bulls.

In the same way, there is a jallikattu going on in all of us as we approach the stage for delivering a performance. It's up to us to demonstrate bravery, expertise and tame the bull reigning in us. The fear might kill us if we don't tame it in time. Just as the jallikattu sportsmen spend years practising to tame the wild bull, we too need to spend years practising and skilling ourselves up to tame the fear to become victorious.

My Fight with the Bull

I have had the opportunity to train more than 55,000 participants worldwide and have addressed more than 2,500 gatherings. God has been good to me and has blessed me with skills to energize, excite and create a lightning impact on the audience. I have coached hundreds of professionals to become high impact presenters and teachers. But even today in spite of all these successes, preparations and practices that I do prior to a program, I still suffer from stage fear. Nervousness creeps through the vein and causes a lot of dismay.

As a primary school student, I once enrolled in the school fest to participate in a storytelling contest. Those days, storytelling also meant the contestants had to narrate the story through words, actions and songs. With immense enthusiasm and support from my parents, I prepared for days.

When I heard my name announced, I rushed onto the stage like other little kids. As I ran up, I stumbled on the wires and fell flat on the stage amidst the laughter of my friends and teachers. Determined I got up and started my story.

I could see the mocking faces and feel the laughter in the auditorium. I became nervous. I was startled and fear reigned over me. My confidence peeled off layer by layer. I felt threatened, defeated and embarrassed. I started but couldn't complete it.

My mind became blank like a whiteboard. John Locke, the philosopher who is known as the 'Father of Liberalism' would call this a state of 'tabula rasa.' I couldn't proceed further; I was overwhelmed by fear and shame. I forgot whatever I had learnt.

Though I had practised so well and had rehearsed many times, as I stood there in front of those ridiculing faces, I became drained and blank. Throat was arid; voice was cracking; hands were trembling; mind reached a state of 'tabula rasa.'

I glanced at my teacher and she looked horribly rude and annoyed. Her piercing look was the last nail and my self-confidence was buried deep instantly. She gestured me to quit the stage.

It was a colossal attack on my self-esteem and from then on till I completed my schooling, I never dared to stand on stage again.

While in college, Dr. MA Abraham, my English Professor and a talented orator, narrated to me the story of a young man who was scared of speaking in public. Once he was invited to deliver a talk to a vegetarian community in London. He prepared and practised well but when the speech started, fear took over. After the first sentence he experienced 'tabula rasa' and couldn't proceed further as fear had utterly taken control of him.

His mind became blank; vision became blurred; voice began to tremble; body started to sweat; people began to scoff. The scar was so deep that for many years he avoided speaking in front of an audience.

Years later as a lawyer, the first case he argued flopped as he couldn't complete the case. He forgot the questions that he had prepared so meticulously. The judge and his fellow advocates mocked him. He ran out of the courtroom painfully humiliated and his self-esteem torn apart.

But he had his fierce determination to tame the bull in him. His determination and passion for a cause that he believed inflamed his resolve and strengthened his courage to bulldoze his fears. He went on to become the Mahatma Gandhi of the world!

Inspiring stories of great heroes can help everyone in his pursuit to overcome the fear of public speaking. I got the ammunition to rebuild my shattered confidence by listening to the heroic acts of visionary leaders.

What Causes Fear?

Have you noticed that people who were afraid once suddenly become fearless? Have you seen that some submissive people all of a sudden become aggressive? Everyone lives a dual personality. We are fearful and fearless at the same time. We are fearful of something and fearless of something else which is more harmful. Hence the first step to overcome fear is to become aware of what we are scared of and identify the reasons for being so.

The book of Judges in the Holy Bible narrates the story of Gideon, a military leader and prophet, who led the people of Israel and protected them from the invasion of the Midianites.

> The first step to overcome fear is to become aware of what we are scared of and identify the reasons for being so.

Israel was under the treacherous rule of Midian. God chose Gideon, the son of Joash from the tribe of Manasseh to save Israel. He led an army of just 300 men against the massive troop of well-trained and well-equipped Midianites. How did he win the war?

Interestingly, Gideon too like the other Israelites, was mightily scared of the Midianites. When God ordered him to rescue the Israelites from the enemies he replied, "How can I rescue Israel? My clan is the weakest tribe of Manasseh and I am the least important member of my family?" Once when God called, he even hid himself because of fear.

Gradually when he began to desert fear, he discovered strength. He started with a large army. But seeing the Midianites who possessed better military strategy and weaponry, his men fled him one by one.

He led an army of fearful men, 32,000 to be precise. God asked him to send away those who were afraid of the Midianites. As soon as he said it, 22,000 deserted instantly. God asked Gideon to choose just 300 brave soldiers from among the 10,000. These 300 who had learnt the art of taming their inner bull ultimately tasted victory!

Gideon's trepidation thus gave way to his triumph. The moment he identified the cause of his fear, he could defeat it and ultimately defeat his enemies. Similarly, if we can list down the reasons for our fears, we too will be able to conquer fear.

What is the real cause of fear: the audience, lack of preparation, lack of confidence or fear of embarrassment? Gideon and his army initially thought the cause of their fear was the huge Midianite army. Soon they identified the reasons for their fear. They were unable to estimate and believe in their own strength.

If one can defeat one's inner fears, one will beat all other fears. The best ruler is one who can rule himself. The moment Gideon and his men learnt this, the size of their troop didn't matter; the size of the enemy didn't matter; what mattered was their resolve to battle their fears.

Tips to Tame the Bull

Everyone knows that communication is a critical skill required to advance in career. In today's corporate battlefield, the winners are those who can convincingly present their ideas and not those who can perform.

One of my most sought-after programs is the training on presentation skills. I have seen that those who can make high-impact presentations have grown up rapidly to enviable positions and cherish a prosperous career.

My book 'Salt and Light' has a chapter dedicated to help the leaders to develop the skills to make high-power presentations. It elaborates on the various stages involved in the designing of content and the skills required to deliver with passion. However, I would like to emphasise once again the importance of overcoming the deadly monster that enslaves us while we are on stage. Fear obstructs our power to succeed.

1. Knowledge is Power

I believe that knowledge is power and those with more knowledge are more powerful. Once we know we are the owners of an immense reservoir of knowledge and we are the masters of the topic fear evades us. Confidence comes by conquering knowledge.

We must spend a considerable amount of time to acquire sufficient knowledge on the topic that we are going to dwell upon. We are not masters of all knowledge. So nothing wrong in asking for time to prepare and rehearse. Ensure to collect a lot of information like a honeybee collecting for posterity.

However believe in the principle of 'less is more'. At times it may pain us to discard what we have collected. Give up the irrelevant information to make a mark. Less is more potent in making an impact.

Thomas Jefferson, the founding father and the third president of USA, has had his influence spread beyond time and history. He could motivate the Americans and was the principal author of the Declaration of Independence. He was brave. But at the same time, he was also diagnosed with a social phobia!

He never managed to deliver his speeches fully. He delivered only two speeches in his long career as

President! He believed in the power of 'less is more'. He would deliver short but powerful messages. This was the secret he used to overcome fear. He also used his writing skills to overcome his weakness. "The most valuable of all talents is that of never using two words when one will do", he says.

"When you are afraid, keep your mind on what you have to do. And if you have been thoroughly prepared, you will not be afraid", says Dale Carnegie.

> Your reputation, credibility and image are created over a period of time. It is not the fruits of hard prayers but hard labour and intense practice!

Once we are ready with high-quality content, the next step is to practice it with precision.

2. Practice Gives Power

This is the best way to defeat fear and tame the bull. Practice gives the ammunition to battle the wild bull. There are topics that I have delivered a hundred times and yet on the previous day of my speech, I prepare again and again.

Good preparation fills us with confidence. It also tells the audience that we respect them. After all, they are investing their precious time to listen to us.

The more we practice, the more impact we create. We are blessed with a lot of good technology today that can help us in practice. We can record our speeches, share them with friends and ask their opinions. For example, I practise standing in front of the mirror. At times, I record my speeches and send it to my friends to get their feedback. This helps me to improve myself.

Practice as if you are in front of a real audience. Practice makes one perfect. Do it in front of your spouse, children or friends to seek their feedback. The fear is the highest just a few seconds before the actual presentation. So practice well to overcome this anxiety. This will also help you to delete the fillers like 'ah', 'oh', 'ok', 'you know' etc. from your speech.

If you have a 30 minutes talk to deliver, ensure you spend minimum of 3 hours on practice. Coming on stage without proper preparation is a crime. Your reputation, credibility and image are created over a period of time. It is not the fruits of hard prayers but hard labour and intense practice!

3. Audience Powers You

We are afraid because we think the audience is smarter, more knowledgeable or more capable than us. This may or may not be true. But remember, if you are on stage, you are better than anyone else. The audience is there to listen to you not to make you fail. They want you to win. They are not your enemies. They want you to succeed as much as you want to succeed yourself.

Look at them as friends and engage with them relaxed and informally. They are there to learn from you not to evaluate you. Give them what they need and they will appreciate you for that.

They don't like monologues; they want a dialogue, a conversation that is rich in knowledge and delivered with empathy and conviction. So involve them as you progress, build rapport and establish a conducive atmosphere for a win-win conclusion.

4. Grooming Gives Power

Our body language, the postures we take, the eye contact we establish, the smile we spread, the energy we reverberate, the passion we display, the tone and pauses we use and even the dress we wear will determine how confident we are going to be while on stage.

The bull inside has to be tamed somehow. While on stage, we either fight or take a flight. The adrenaline reveals itself in symptoms like a pale face, dry mouth, faster heartbeat, blank mind, shaky legs and soaked palms. However, a good grooming can monitor these ill effects and keep our heartbeat under control.

What we wear tells who we are and how we feel about ourselves. "The apparel proclaims the man", says Shakespeare. This helps to create the best impact and overcome stage fear. We need to invest in our appearance. We need to learn the skill of dressing and grooming.

We are fortunate! There are numerous masters who teach us the art of grooming. Warren Buffet leads a prosperous career. But as a student, he felt terribly afraid to stand in front of people. He overcame this by taking it head-on. Though initially he was known to avoid the stage, he realized to become successful he had to tame the bull. So he enrolled himself for a professional presentation skills course, learnt the tricks and went on to become one of the richest men in history.

5. Power of Movements

Stagnation kills. A motionless monotonous monster can kill hundreds in a few seconds with his stale talk. One technique that I use to defeat fear is that of movements.

Try to move your hands, use gestures, take a good posture and move around confidently with your chest out and head straight when you are on stage next time. You will experience the magic!

Our posture determines our attitude. How we stand, look, walk and move will radiate positive energy and confidence. Body language matters a lot in demonstrating a confident appearance. Exhibit the correct body language while on stage.

The most important tool that we have is our hands. Often we waste them by hiding it at the back or in the pockets. These postures reveal our incompetence and lack of confidence. Use the hands to make a point; use them to list the points; use them to dramatize and create visuals in the minds of the audience.

Let me tell you two more secrets that helped me to tame the bull. Breathe. Smile.

Every time you are on stage, breathe in and out slowly, deeply and gently to overcome social anxiety and fear. Smile as you breathe. Smile more and more, so that your listeners will believe you love their presence.

The Power of Demosthenes

Do you know that the power of an orator is greater than the power of a king? Demosthenes, the Greek statesman, who lived in the 4th century BC, was one of the most famous political orators in history. Like many other achievers, he too faced immense challenges in early life. He was afflicted with stammering and faced ridicule everywhere he went.

When he realized the power of public speaking, he decided to give his best to become one. The stammering choked him. The ridicules destroyed his spirits. It is said that he would practice with pebbles in his mouth and recite poetries as he ran on the beaches shouting over the roar of the waves. He would run up and down the mountains shouting out long sentences. Gradually he won the war over his weakness.

He gave his first speech at the age of 20 and went on to become one of the best influencers and constructors of democracy. He exhorted the Athenians to oppose king Philip of Macedon and his son Alexander the Great.

His speeches were so powerful that King Philip once remarked, "You may conquer the whole world, but you cannot defeat Demosthenes in speech."

As we said earlier, the power of a leader lies to a large extent in his communication and oratorial skills. Look at any leader that you know and you will realize that his power rests in his speech!

We are Prisoners of Fear

I have been inspired much by the stories of Brian Cavanaugh. In his book the Sower's Seeds, he narrates the story of the prisoners.

The prisoners were given the task of completing a new prison. The modern prison was to replace the old one that had housed hundreds of prisoners for decades.

After the construction of the new prison the prisoners were given the task of demolishing the old one. Under the supervision of the guards, they began to tear down the old prison.

> "The best medicine for stage fear is to go on stage and fight it out."
> Andrea Bocelli

While dismantling the jail walls, the prisoners were shocked and infuriated to find that although the grills were made of heavy steel bars and had a massive lock on them, the walls of the cells were made of paper and clay painted to resemble stone and iron. It became apparent to them that if they had pushed the wall a bit, it would have fallen down and would have helped them to escape.

For years they had huddled in their locked prisons, thinking escape was impossible. No one ever tried it because it seemed that freedom was beyond their reach.

Like these prisoners, we too are imprisoned by our fears. A small push, a gentle effort, a little preparation is all that we need to break the walls of our prisons and liberate ourselves. We had been huddled inside the prison of fear and believed liberation from fear was impossible.

When we run away from fear, it runs behind us, not with us. The best way to battle is to battle it like the Jallikattu artist. "The best medicine for stage fear is to go on stage and fight it out", says Andrea Bocelli, the Italian tenor and instrumentalist who became blind as a child.

Many of us need a push. Fear chains us down. We must take the bull on its horn and tame it with courage. We too can tame the bull!

The Path to Immortality

Om, asato ma sad gamaya

Tamaso ma jyotir gamaya

Mrtyor ma amrtam gamaya,

Om Santi, Santi, Santih

Om, from the unreal lead me to the Real

From darkness lead me to Light

From death lead me to Immortality

Om Santi, Santi, Santih

Brihadaranyaka Upanishad

Give Your Best to be the Best

The only way to become the best is to give the best in whatever one does. "If a man is called to be a street sweeper, he should sweep streets even as Michelangelo painted or Beethoven composed music or Shakespeare wrote poetry. He should sweep streets so well that all the hosts of heaven and earth will pause to say, 'Here lived a great street sweeper who did his job well," says Martin Luther King.

It doesn't matter the type of work we do; what matters is the intention and the commitment with which we do it. This will make us the best.

> When people talk about our good works and our good intentions, we become immortal!

If we wish to 'leave footprints on the sands of time' and leave this world with people fondly remembering us long after we have gone, then we need to give the best in whatever we do. When people talk about our good works and our good intentions, we become immortal!

Not the best words, but actions done with the best intentions will bring us laurels. There are too many preachers using the best and the most convincing vocabulary but the world today needs people who can bring out the best action. Words without action mean nothing. The world needs people who can give, for we have far too many takers.

Being an African-American, young Booker found it very difficult to get a seat in any of the Universities in US. When he heard of a University that admitted coloured students like him he walked four hundred miles to reach the place only to hear that the college was already full. After much pleading, they gave him the post of a sweeper.

He did his job so meticulously and passionately that the authorities were pleased and admitted him  soon as a student. Later this boy became the principal of the University of Tuskegee and one of the finest men in the world. Booker T. Washington achieved this position by giving his best in whatever he did.

I had many fantastic opportunities to work with people who performed their roles and responsibilities with the highest levels of commitment. Vinoth was one of them. He was in charge of administration and data management in our team. He would be in office before we reached and leave long after we left. This type of commitment was rare among the youth of those days.

After two years of dedicated service, he resigned as he got another offer as a safety officer in an organization.

During the farewell, he narrated an amazing story that touched everyone.

After completing his diploma, since he couldn't find a job due to the recession of 2009, he joined our company on contract as a housekeeping boy. His role included activities like cleaning the toilets. He took up this job and worked there for a year. He displayed immense commitment and dedication at work.

He was doing his work so well that some managers from production noticed him and slowly began to appreciate him and converse with him. In one such discussion, one of the leaders realized that this young boy deserved a better job as he had completed his diploma in engineering. So he was recruited for the HRD as an admin staff. His dedication to work amazed us. Vinoth currently leads a team of safety officers in a reputed organization.

We have scores of such success stories of people going from rags to riches. However, there is something common in all of them: their willingness to do everything in the best possible way they could. They believed that excellence didn't come from the type of work they did, but from the way they did their work, however menial it might be.

When the performer takes pride in his work and does it to the best of his ability, excellence comes. Whether washing floors, building a house, driving a car, making a car or heading the most profitable organization, success depends on our dedication.

If we give our best in our activities people will admire us. When we do our best, we will achieve success beyond imagination. Doing our best in whatever we do is the secret to a happy life.

What Prevents You from Giving Your Best?

In a recent survey, I asked my participants, "What stops you from giving your best?"

The answers matched what I had assumed. "My boss doesn't permit me to perform"; "My boss is not transparent and helpful"; "There is no budget"; "Too much of hierarchy in my team"; "Unclear expectations from management"; "No appreciation for the good work done"; "No role clarity".

All opinions were directed outward. Everyone blamed someone else. No one was willing to take responsibility for the inferior performance.

"It's not because of me." "Let the others change first and then I shall change." "I am eager to do well; but the politics in my team is not permitting me to perform." "This leadership program is excellent, but will be more suitable for my bosses." "This book on self-development is apt for the young workers."

We all love to blame others though we know that a blamer will only get marooned. It is time that we identify the real cause of our complacency and inferior performance. The root cause is inside us. Throwing mud at others will make us dirtier. Excuses exhaust us.

External causes will always be there. They don't vanish with our wishes. Those who weed out the inner cause of non-performance will accelerate towards superior performance. Looking inwardly to find solutions to problems is the sign of a new age professional.

1. From Ordinary to Extraordinary

Vinoth performed his routine tasks with passion, care and dedication. We become mediocre and ordinary people when we do things ordinarily. When we perform our duties with the best intention and utmost commitment, even if we are doing ordinary things, we become extraordinary people. Doing ordinary things extraordinarily will win us many trophies in life and will make us legends.

The ingredients of ownership are self-reliance, personal initiative, imagination, enthusiasm, self-discipline, willingness to give more, to go beyond work timings and take up additional responsibilities etc. These people become like talent magnets that attract success and growth in the organization.

> Doing ordinary things extraordinarily will win us many trophies in life and will make us legends.

When ownership is low, productivity is low; but absenteeism, militancy and disharmony are high. On the other hand, when ownership is high, people get noticed immediately.

In 1962 John F Kennedy went to visit Nasa. As he entered, he saw a person cleaning the floors. Kennedy being an affectionate leader, went to the man to introduce himself. "I am John F Kennedy, the President of the United States of America. And what do you do?" He asked him.

The man looked at Kennedy and replied, "I am helping a man to get to the moon."

This is the pride that all of us should have in whatever we do. He equally felt proud that he was part of a great mission and was not just a labourer cleaning the floors. He felt that his role as a sweeper contributed to his nation's goals. This is the pride we should possess in our work, big or small.

2. Work with Clear Goals

When we have an aim, we give our best to achieve it. All great achievers were people with goals, and it kept them alive and active in their work. We need to have goals in life if we want to give our best and achieve anything in life.

Achievers have some big ideas and they totally commit themselves to those ideas. They do everything with the best intention and that helps them to leave behind a legacy. To do anything well, we too must have a goal, commit ourselves to it and fall in love with it. Our goals motivate us, challenge us and push us to give our best.

Steve Martin, actor and writer, born in a wealthy family, led a goalless life as a youngster. He began his career at Disneyland where he sold guidebooks. In his free time he frequented a magician to learn magic and soon got the job as a magician at the Fantasyland of Disney. He soon quit this job and joined a comedy troupe. But he couldn't stick there too.

He went on to study philosophy and theatre at the insistence of his friends. However he soon dropped out of college as studies disenchanted him.

> "Become so good that no one can ignore you."
> Steve Martin

So he began to focus on writing and acting. His standup comedy shows became huge hits and he had to perform at large stadiums to satisfy the crowd. He won five Grammy awards, Primetime Emmy award and a life achievement award. "What will make anyone successful?" People asked him. "The secret is to become so good in your goal that no one can ignore you", he answered.

3. Limitations are Opportunities

Walt Disney's cartoons were rejected by publishers until he created Mickey Mouse. Edison was considered too stupid to learn until he astonished the world with his inventions. Our failures are stepping stones towards our goals and so we should never be afraid of them. We just do our best and hope for the best. When we do the best, failures will soon turn into successes.

We need to convert our failures into our opportunities. All of us have a share of defects. But we should never allow these defects to control us. Ludwig van Beethoven, the German composer, was deaf and yet composed some of the most melodious music in the world. John Milton the renowned intellectual poet who wrote 'Paradise Lost', considered as the greatest literary piece in the world, was blind. Abraham Lincoln was poor and yet he became one of the greatest US presidents.

If you believe in yourself and do your best, you will go beyond your limitations and your failures will become your opportunities. So give your best even when you go through tough weather.

Fear of failure is the thorn that pierces our feet as we run to success. Failure is like a shadow that refuses to leave us. "Never fear the shadows. They simply mean there is a light shining somewhere nearby", says Ruth E Renkel, a popular German writer.

4. Become the Owner of Your Work

I give my participants a challenge while I facilitate the program on 'Ownership and Accountability'. I ask them to sign their signatures with their right hand first. Then I ask them to sign with their left hand. Whether they like it or not, both are their signatures. The signature, signed by the left hand, may not look so neat. However this is theirs anyway.

In the same way, it's possible that we may not like some of our works. But we must take ownership because it's our work and we alone are hired to do that. The work given to us may not be up to our expectations; maybe we are much more qualified and experienced; yet it's our work.

When we do the small tasks with commitment and passion, bigger tasks will come our way. It does not matter what we do; what matters is how we do, the spirit with which we do these small things of life. Chung Ju Yung, the founder of Hyundai says, "Those who are honest and sincere in doing simple and small things will also be sincere and honest in doing big things." In other words, if we give our best, the best will come to us.

5. Never Say Die

Today we live in a world which lacks ethics and principles. We think to be successful we need to be street smart. Sometimes we sacrifice our principles to get what we want. We need to give our best according to the principles of our hearts.

'Be all that you can be', is the recruitment slogan of US army. It doesn't mean that we become perfect or we outperform others. It is a simple invitation to give one's best in what one does. It is a challenge to rise above one's abilities and surprise oneself by going beyond one's limits. To do our best, we need to develop a never-say-die attitude and commit to give our best at all times.

Enthusiasm is an important ingredient to become the best. High performers exhibit a lot of enthusiasm, positive energy and excitement. "Enthusiasm is the match that lights the candle of achievement", says William Arthur Ward. It gives one the spirit of never giving up and the determination to push ahead in spite of hardships.

6. Nishkama Karma

Bhagavat Gita says, "Keep doing what you believe in, what you know is right without expecting and worrying about what you get in return." We must do our best not for getting titles and honours, but because of the fulfilment and satisfaction it brings. To give our best is in our human nature.

We must learn to do things without expecting any benefits in return. We do our best to turn us into the best human being.

Our organizations need people who are sincere and honest, who are willing to give their maximum. Many of us behave like the mice that play when the cat is absent. Just look around our offices: no work is done, no commitments are met, no customers are satisfied, breaks become longer and more frequent and nothing significant happens when the boss is on leave. It proclaims our personality. We project ourselves to be immature people who always need guidance, control and supervision.

The best organizations are those where the members go on working whether the supervisor is present or not. We act like slaves who need supervision to become effective. It is a shame that we become more productive when our supervisors give us feedback and monitor us. As a result organizations go on strengthening the hierarchy by hiring more bosses above us. The best works are done not to please the bosses but to feel justified before one's conscience.

> "We cannot do great things, but only small things with great love."
> Mother Teresa

All of us have certain roles to perform in our organizations. These are the best roles assigned to us who are the best to handle them. We are hired and paid for doing these roles. Our company will become the best if we give our best. When our company becomes the best, we become the best.

We need to do our best instead of waiting for others to do their best. It does not mean we wait for extraordinary things to come by to start performing. Just do ordinary things in an extraordinary way! "We cannot do great things, but only small things with great love", says Mother Teresa.

Those who rise above mediocrity and give twice as much as he should be giving, will never be ignored. I love the shopkeeper who gives me 'a little more'. I am his loyal customer.

People will notice if we work a little harder, if we take charge of the situations, if we give solutions to problems, if we are a little more kind, compassionate and considerate. People will notice us!

It is said that every organization has four bones. The wishbone: wishing somebody would do something about the problem; the jawbones: doing all the talking and doing nothing else; the knucklebones: those who knock everything and knock down everybody else; and the backbone: those who carry the brunt of the load and do most of the work.

If you want to be the best, become the backbone. This will help you to stand out, firm and strong. Become so good that no one can ignore you!

2 Noble Works for Noble People

One of the earliest lessons we learnt in school is that 'every work is noble.' However, we never grasped its real meaning and continued to live our days grumbling, unhappy and unproductive and longed for the noblest job to come. But that noble job rarely arrived.

When we realize that every work is noble and the worker, irrespective of the type of work he does, is also noble, we begin to enjoy the thrill, challenge and excitement of work. In this way, we become noble people.

"God gives us nuts but he doesn't crack them," says an Irish proverb. The world is not a finished product. We contribute to it through our sincere work to make it more perfect and ideal. We work to bring out a new earth. This new earth will arrive when our works promote a better order in society, uphold human dignity and promote love, equality, freedom and creativity.

In this process, we also perfect ourselves and thus our work becomes a means for our self-actualization.

Our aim and efforts should not be to produce better things only but to bring out better people in a better world. The aim of life is flowering of persons and not perfectioning of things. The ultimate purpose is to build high quality individuals and not high quality products.

What is Work?

It is difficult to define work because what is work for one may be hobby for another, a punishment for someone and a passion for someone else. "Work is a human life activity whose purposes are the production of goods and services necessary for human subsistence. It's the realization of human abilities and capabilities", says PA Peter, educationist and social activist from Assam. Humans through work unfold their creative energy.

Works are important because through work we humanize nature and the universe, fulfill our goals, develop our talents and potentials, maintain and promote our lives, become united with one another and humbly serve each other. Our work makes us better human beings while unemployment may dehumanize us.

> Our work makes us better human beings while unemployment may dehumanize us.

We develop our character by earning things not by getting them for nothing. Everything in life has to be earned. The only thing we get free is our life. Our works also help us to achieve satisfaction, enjoy the sweetness of success and lead us on to self-actualization.

Our works make us happy and keep us alive. Our works help us to enjoy the dignity of labour and the pleasure of accomplishment.

Work can promote independence, responsibility and interpersonal sensitivities. It gives us endurance, humility and love for progress. It is the only medicine for sorrow and loneliness. It is the only path to success and fame. It is our karma marga, our path to the life eternal. Work is an essential part of being human.

Work makes us human and divine!

The Negative Consequences of Work

According to Karl Marx, work creates alienation. First there is the worker and then there are his products. The product is separated from the producer and they do not belong to him once the production is completed.

The product that he so passionately produced loses his control and authority once he sells the products. Simply said, others have control over one's knowledge and product and as a result one feels alienated from what one created.

Another adverse effect is the devaluation of the person. Our world is too much product oriented.

In such a product oriented society, my worth is measured on the parameters of my productivity and usefulness. If I am able to contribute to a product, then I have value otherwise, my existence is of no use.

I am defined by the work I do, more than the person that I am. If I deliver results and contribute to the goals of the organization I am valued, rewarded and recognized. If not I am devalued and fired.

Organizations are in a mad rush to hire millennials and are in a hurry to replace experience and loyalty with new blood and fresh thinking. A conscious bias against the aged workforce is present in most places. The older generation, as Karl Marx said, feels alienated and threatened by the new generation parochial leaders, who advocate a 'use and throw' culture.

"We encounter selfish lifestyles marked by an opulence which is no longer sustainable and frequently indifferent to the world around us. To our dismay, we see the technical and economic questions dominating political debate to the detriment of genuine concern for human beings. Men and women risk being reduced to mere cogs in a machine that treats them as items of consumption to be exploited", says Pope Francis, the head of the Catholic Church and an active voice on behalf of the dignity of the worker.

Human beings as co-creators of this world should work to acquire the means to live a good life. This work is for the good of society not for its detriment. However when workers are exploited and used as a means to create profit, unrest broods among the workers and they stand up for social justice.

Leaders are stewards not masters. They have a personal obligation to care for the team, for the organization and the society. Their goals are not targets and profits alone. They have to help people to build their dreams and help them to progress in life. A steward creates a heaven by treating all as equals. He has the responsibility to help the workers to come out of the negative consequences of work.

Rest is Right

Every worker has a right to rest. Even gods took rest after work and war. Holy Bible, for example, says that God worked for six days and took

> While our works give us the breath to survive, the rest we have is the fuel for the work.

rest on the 7th day. Work and rest were part of Gods' schedule. God worked in the heavens and He rested. We also follow the same pattern to foster a heavenly experience here on earth.

We too work for 5 or 6 days and rest for a day. This is work-life balance. Work is more important than rest; rest is a right only for those who work. Vacation and leisure are good but work is better. Even for the richest man, the thought of losing his job is a nightmare because all of us are designed to work.

Some people think we work to earn and survive. It is true. We work so that we will survive, for without work we will perish. While our works give us the breath to survive, the rest we have is the fuel for the work.

Every Work is Noble

There is no debate that work is necessary and every work is noble. It all depends on our attitude. It is something that is natural to human beings. But due to our selfish ambitions and interests it is seen as laborious, oppressive, fatiguing and arduous.

We need to alter our attitude to work. The quality of our work is directly related to the quality of our attitude, mind and intentions.

Some soldiers were trying to push a wagon stuck in the mud. Their corporal gave orders, but did not lend  a hand. They just needed one more person's support to make the wagon to move. A man came along and watched the scene. He asked the corporal why he did not help the soldiers.

"I am a corporal! How can I! These are my subordinates."

The man got down from his horse, took off his coat, rolled up the sleeves, helped the soldiers and they easily pulled the wagon out. As the man mounted onto his horse to leave, he pulled out a visiting card from his wallet, gave it to the corporal and said, "The next time you have such a problem don't hesitate to call me." And he saddled off.

The corporal glanced at the card and found on it written: 'George Washington, the President of the United States of America'.

This story that I learnt in my Moral Science class as a school student still inspires me to believe that every work is noble. This thought is not new. People in all cultures considered work as noble. The Greeks believed that through work people imitated God the creator. The Romans believed that work well done could merit rewards in the next world. In the Christendom, works were considered as worship and the worker was a co-creator with God.

In India, from Vedic times onwards, work was considered as normal to human beings. All human beings come from Purusha and all activities are from him alone. But as time passed, the caste system came in and some works were considered lower than the other works.

Bhagavad Gita encourages people to do activities imitating Krishna who himself is a working God. Indian philosophy suggests Karma Marga as one of the ways to attain salvation. Work is to be done for the sake of work without any desire for benefits. Only such a nishkama karma can liberate people and make them noble.

Many modern philosophers consider work as a necessary evil or as a punishment. Some Greek philosophers believed that work was a curse. For example, Aristotle considered unemployment as a more worthy life than employment because work for him was a punishment.

But if we look at it positively, we will realize that it is part of God's plan. Our works make us blessed. Work is good for human beings just as it was good for God. We participate in the creative act of God through our works. It enhances human dignity. We are hired to become a steward.

We discover our meaning and purpose in life through our work. Imagine a life where you have all wealth but no work to do. It would be the most horrific life!

When we look at our work as a means to glorify ourselves, as a tool to earn money, to become

> Our works make us fully human and fully alive. There is no better worship than doing our duty with utmost sincerity, commitment and passion.

powerful or use it to exalt our superiority we lose the authentic dignity of work. In this process, we lose our dignity and our work loses its nobility.

We become enslaved to the fruits of our work. Our intentions enslave and limit us. In such cases, our works are far from being noble.

"Excellence comes when we take pride in our work and believe that every work is noble. We must do what we have to do with the utmost diligence, care and love and then our work will bring us joy, satisfaction and will become a means for our self-actualization", says Jaimon Joseph who has spent more than three decades working for the under-privileged and the oppressed in different parts of India.

As we said, skills are necessary and essential for success. But skills without goodness cannot make us noble. The purity of heart, the genuine intention to transform the world and sincere acts of goodness can make our work noble.

Our works make us fully human and fully alive. There is no better worship than doing our duty with utmost sincerity, commitment and passion. Half-hearted effort will produce only half-finished products and half-lively people. Nobility stays far away from them.

Become Visible or Invisible: Your Choice

An executive of a renowned multinational training NGO once told me that he wouldn't leave his less-paid job for a fatter pay, because his present organization gave him visibility and respect. It is a fact that there are people who look for visibility more than remuneration. If their organizations give them that they will stay on giving their best.

Visibility can be within or outside the organization. Many of us do very well in our work but few of us get noticed. If we have done something well, we have every right to get noticed in the organization. We must make it a habit to get ourselves noticed and our presence felt in the place where we work.

People who make their successes and works visible get the reward while those who keep them invisible become invisible themselves.

Often I meet a few individuals, irrespective of the changes at the top leadership, they always remain popular, as their views are sought out by the leadership. Not that they do things differently. Not that they are more talented or more committed than the rest. Not that they do something impressive or massive. They just know how to get noticed.

Not everyone is great at brand building. However the good news is that it's a skill that everyone can master. So here are some tips to become more visible.

1. Demonstrate that You Give Your Maximum

The best way to get noticed is to give one's maximum in whatever one does. We all do our work sincerely. But we miss out on one thing: displaying our works to those who matter. High performers are 'maximum givers' but visibility does not come from this alone. We need to learn the art of developing the right network with people who matter and communicate with them regularly about our high performance. If we do so, we will always be respected and rewarded.

We must not only give our whole heart, energy and talents to our tasks but must also advertise it wholeheartedly. When we do things with total commitment and full passion our work will produce maximum output and we will be recognized for our achievements.

Many organizations have titles like 'employee of the month', 'employee of the year', 'core talent or high pots' etc. to reward and recognize the high performers. But these titles go to those who are visible. It isn't enough that we give our best; we must also tell people that we are giving our best.

How often do we hold a one-on-one meeting with our reporting head? He might be busy and is not a prophet to read our minds. But if we want visibility ask for an appointment to talk to him at least once a month.

Your work plans, career and personal goals, development requirements, aspirations and achievements must be part of this meeting's agenda. Request him for more challenging assignments that you think will help you gain visibility in the organization. Tell him with respect if you feel your talents are unutilized in the current role.

Talk to him at par like two adults. You are not inferior to him in anyway. If you feel you are sidelined or excluded from important projects, make him aware of that. Ask him for suggestions and guidance to improve your image and executive presence.

> Don't get trapped at your workstation or in your little cubicles.

Give him suggestions to improve his role and also speak positively about his support to you. At the end of the day, our happiness, our career and our visibility lie to a large extent in his hands. So foster a good relationship with the leader.

2. Management by Walking Around

This is a simple way to get noticed. Some of us become too serious about the works that we fail to see our colleagues and bosses. We may do beautiful things but if we do not have the required human relation skills, then we will never be noticed.

It doesn't mean we trumpet all our successes all the time but we need to share our accomplishments with those who matter in the organization. It is important to communicate with our bosses often and tell them what we have done.

The principle of management by walking around in the office can be practised by all. We are not alone in our company. There are many others who too are doing wonderful things. Don't get trapped at your workstation or marooned in your little cubicles. We need to get up from our seats and go around meeting people, chatting with them and learning from them or at least to offer them a smile. Meeting others will always give us fresh ideas, refresh our enthusiasm and make us visible and lovable.

3. Exhibit Energy and Enthusiasm

People love those with high energy and enthusiasm. A barrel of vinegar cannot attract even a single fly. Display positive spirit, high energy, zeal and enthusiasm if you want to get noticed. This will enhance your personality and people will love coming to you. However, this doesn't mean you have the license to mock at people, put them down or make fun of them.

People think talking loud and loose is a sign of confidence. Not necessarily. Empty vessels make more noise. Genuine interest in people coupled with a warm welcoming and open attitude will make you visible.

Years ago, I had the opportunity to coach a young zonal head of a Pharma company. He was a bundle of energy. He told me that he is on business trips from Monday to Saturday, travelling across South India to promote his products and motivate his team. He would achieve his targets pretty well too.

In spite of the pressures of work, targets, travel and leading his team, when he reaches home on Saturday evening, he manages his own laundry, ironing and packing for his next trip. In addition he is fully involved in Church activity on Sundays and is an active member and leader of many associations serving society.

The more energy and enthusiasm we display the more time we gain, the more successful and happier we become. People with high energy, zeal and enthusiasm always find extra time to do a little more than others. They always have time for new things and new friends. In the process, they get noticed.

4. Accept, Admire and Appreciate

If you want admiration, admire others first. We not only trumpet our achievements and capabilities but also need to appreciate and admire the achievements and potentials of our colleagues and bosses.

We must respect others and speak positively about them. We must talk positively about our company

> We need to treat people not merely as means of production but as opportunities with immense capabilities and potentials.

and must feel proud to belong to it. Positive people always have more visibility and they will always be sought after by others.

Appreciate sincerely the contributions of others especially of your colleagues and subordinates not only the bosses. It is always better to appreciate people in public and correct them in private. Make sure to include appreciative vocabulary in your routine conversations. Appreciate everyone, every time and everywhere, if you want to become visible.

The greatest asset at our disposal is the human resource. We need to treat people not merely as means of production but as opportunities with immense capabilities and potential. We need to believe in people and in their power. When we begin to view them as treasures of great possibilities and respect them for what they are we become visible.

We must also remember that we can't rise by pulling down others. We must fight for our due credit but don't covet the honours that belong to others. People won't go far by stealing the glory of others.

Organization wants its success not yours. Helping others is the surest way for us to become successful. So if we steal what belongs to others and don't give their due then we will not reach anywhere.

5. Immerse in Initiatives

One of the best ways to get visibility is to take up initiatives. Leaders are self-made and so we have plenty of opportunities in our organizations to take up initiatives to become leaders.

Volunteering and becoming part of unique projects and teams will help us get noticed. Another way to become visible is to join groups and clubs within the organization. If we communicate well our ideas, take up initiatives without waiting for the manager to delegate. Speak up during meetings; demonstrate expertise; volunteer for new projects; deal fairly with people. These will get you noticed.

If you look around your organization, you will find that those successful are part of some task force teams, special committees and projects. They readily accept any challenging tasks and are proactive in their conversations with their leaders. They volunteer themselves to take up additional responsibilities. These initiatives give them recognition and visibility.

Make sure you use the usual channels like the newsletter, notice boards, social media etc. where you can post articles with your name attached to them. This too will give you visibility. In one of my earlier organizations we had two pillars called the pillar of appreciation and the pillar of ideas on which everyone was encouraged to write an appreciation note about someone else, or write some innovative quotes and ideas. These helped to gain visibility.

6. Humility Makes One Visible

When we are humble, we are visible. This is one of the best ways to become visible in any organization, in society and even in family. Humility doesn't mean we are quiet and timid. It doesn't mean we never talk about our accomplishments. Instead, it is our ability to accept our mistakes and give credit to others for their successes.

We are in a false trend today, which says, 'those who can talk big will also act big.' Sadly, there are many who talk of big things, big ideas and complex jargons, often stolen from management books, but very few who really do something.

> The tray of humility serves peace, patience, kindness, compassion, forbearance, joy, love and wisdom.

"If we wish to reach the highest peak of humility and soon arrive at the heavenly heights, we must by our good deeds set up a ladder like the Jacob's upon which he saw the angels climbing up and down. We go up by humbling and go down by praising ourselves", says St. Benedict in his book The Rules.

The tray of humility serves peace, patience, kindness, compassion, forbearance, joy, love and wisdom. It helps us to accept the bread of affliction and the wine of remorse. It makes us visible!

If you want to be noticed don't go around saying blah, blah. Instead stop talking and begin to do some actions. Only the great display the virtue of humility. "God has two thrones. One in the highest heavens, the other in the lowliest heart", says DL Moody, writer and theologian.

7. Discipline Defines Destiny

People who are punctual, responsible, disciplined and helpful are always visible. If your swipe-in time is 8.00 am, make sure you are there at your seat by 7.45 am.

Are you the last one to rush in for meetings after it has started? Do you make people to wait for you? Do you keep your commitments and promises? Do you follow a routine or face the day as it comes up? Do you answer your phone calls or emails immediately? Do you wear the attire as demanded by the company including the PPEs? The answers to these questions tell us how disciplined we are.

We need to be more responsible with regard to the use of our time, resources and talents. We need to keep our places clean, protect the assets of the company and support our colleagues who are struggling to complete a task. These deeds may look simple but leave an indelible mark about our character. They determine our destiny!

8. Good Deeds Give Visibility

Shillong, the capital of Meghalaya, is called the 'Scotland of the East'. One of the most enchanting drives that I would enjoy was the one from Upper Shillong to Chirapunjee. We experience the enthralling beauty of nature as we begin the drive. The road is scenic with tall pine trees aesthetically planted on either side. The beauty stretches for miles.

As you drive along you begin to wonder who was that noble soul who planted these pine trees which today give immense beauty to the landscape. The trees were planted nearly 100 years ago by an Italian Christian missionary who worked in the region. When he was planting those saplings some people laughed at his idea. "You will never live enough to see these trees grow up" they said. "I want to do something useful to society. The future generation will enjoy the benefits of this labour", he seemed to have replied.

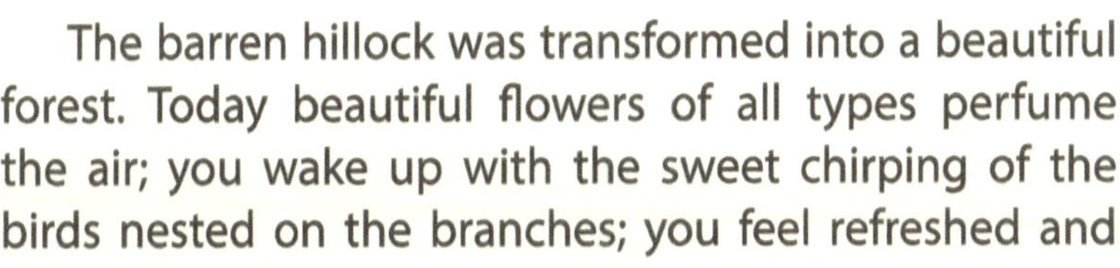

The barren hillock was transformed into a beautiful forest. Today beautiful flowers of all types perfume the air; you wake up with the sweet chirping of the birds nested on the branches; you feel refreshed and re-energized as you drive along the long stretch of the road decorated by the mighty trees that guard you on both sides of the road.

The good deed done by a noble soul has outlived him and bears testimony to the fact that any deed done with the best intention will be recognized someday. "Always give without remembering and always receive without forgetting", says Brian Tracy, author and leadership coach.

While we try to build up our personal brand, we must be careful to tread softly and gently so as not to damage the brands and images of our colleagues. Sometime ago, I worked with a colleague who was excellent in building his personal brand. He used every opportunity to promote himself and would convince us that it was for the team's benefit.

> Getting recognized at work and becoming visible is the responsibility of the individual.

Initially, the team believed him. Soon we saw through his malicious intentions and the moment we realized that he was solely interested to promote his personal brand and not the team's brand, we stopped collaborating and he fell from status immediately.

Small men like this use others to build their brand. However it becomes a futile act.

Remember we live in a battlefield! Doing work sincerely and remaining quite about it will get us nowhere. All of us should learn the skills to raise our visibility at work.

We work very hard, meet the targets beyond expectations and are professionals at work. We at times skip our meals to complete a task or complete a meeting, even go home late because of our commitment to work. We take the work home and continue to work on our weekends.

We do everything and yet we live invisible lives at the workplace and when it is time for promotions, praises or rewards, we lose out.

Getting recognized at work and becoming visible is the responsibility of the individual. As we said, it is a skill that all can master and there are innumerable ways to learn it. The million-dollar question is whether we are willing to make a choice. We can be visible or invisible in our organizations. The choice is ours.

4 It's Your Work, Own It, Man!

The success of an organization is directly proportional to the ownership mindset of its employees. Vipin Sachdev, the CEO of Pink Papaya Foods, that owned the franchisee of Subway in Chennai, has been a leader who inspires ownership among his employees. He believes in the goodness of people and encourages his employees to think that the company belongs to them. "Don't just act like an owner, you must also think like the owner. Think that this company belongs to you. If you think like the owner, one day you will own a company", he encourages them.

In order to inculcate this spirit of ownership, he keeps aside enough budget for training and gives immense focus on employee motivation and empowerment. In fact, the first half of every day, his managers spend their time attending training on ownership, leadership and intrapreneurship. He believes that high performance is the fruit of ownership and accountability.

One of the ways by which he instils ownership in his employees is by explaining to them clearly what success means. Many employees think that they work to make the company richer. He believes that it is crucial to show them how their work impacts their future.

He begins with the why and then shows them how they are connected to this why. The why can be sales targets, customer retention, customer delight or opening of more restaurants. He spends hours explaining how their contributions are valuable to achieve this goal. He inspires a purpose in life and challenges them to discover why they do what they do.

The employees understand and accept the purpose of what they do. As a result, they assume ownership of their jobs and become motivated and engaged. They feel proud to work in a place where their works significantly affect the company's outcome.

> People who take up ownership are trusted by their leaders and customers.

Most leaders make their teams feel inferior to them. They treat them like workers and they act like the owners. It is true that employees cannot be the owner. But they can take ownership of their work. We are fortunate that we still have visionary and selfless leaders like Vipin. Today, many of those managers who worked with him lead their own businesses both in India and abroad.

How to Take up Ownership?

"It's not my company. Whatever I do, I am still a worker. Why should I take ownership?" People ask these questions during trainings.

The best way to exhibit ownership of a job is by taking up initiatives. We lose many opportunities to act and grow because we wait for someone to take the lead. We think someone has to tell us to do this and that. People with an ownership mindset will not wait for directions. They act first and become responsible for their act.

Some people wait for resources, some for the right time and some for the right people to do something. A sense of ownership inspires one to take up the initiative without waiting for directions because one believes it is good for the organization. People who take up ownership are trusted by their leaders and customers.

A leader in an ownership culture inspires people to make the right choice daily: to choose between doing nothing or doing something. He has to create a safe atmosphere for people to share ideas and in turn he has to show that he is excited to listen to their new ideas. If we don't have time to listen to everyone's ideas, create a platform or a process so that people can share their ideas and thoughts.

There are leaders who say, "You are always welcome to my office to share your ideas and concerns." However, though they make such tall promises, these leaders are seldom accessible to ordinary employees and their offices are always shut or guarded by heavy securities.

Tomorrow never comes. Initiatives have to be taken today. We all wait for the perfect time, perfect ideas and perfect people. But alas, perfection is always an idea of a utopian world. Start today with your idea and don't wait for tomorrow. Owners don't wait for the right time to take initiatives. They overcome the tendency to procrastinate and consider today as the best day to start.

Ownership is expressed through volunteering. However, the problem with many leaders is that they reward people who volunteer to perform critical tasks. All leaders must do that. At the same time, there are so many unsung heroes, who volunteer to support these 'declared heroes'. We need to recognize them as well. This is one way by which we can create an ownership culture.

Accountability

Ownership also gets its expression in accountability. This means we are responsible for the outcome: both successes and failures. It is about getting everyone committed to the goal. It is the assurance that you give to your team and organization that you will deliver what you promised; that you will accept your failures and protect your team if the goals are not achieved.

> Accountability is not forced upon; rather it is a commitment that one freely makes to get the results that one wants.

While accountability is assigned and given to the employees by the manager, ownership is taken by the employee. A leader can't appoint ownership. Rather, he can create the right environment for the employees to volunteer to do a challenging task or take up an important assignment. People who take up ownership will take up the initiatives to solve the problems they find on the way.

In an ownership culture, a leader's role is to inspire ownership. In such a culture, the employees take pride in making things happen. They feel it's their work, their responsibility, their decisions, their ideas and their challenges. These are people with an 'ours-mindset.'

"Something happens when you take ownership. You no longer act like a spectator or consumer, because you are an owner", says Bob Goff, motivational speaker and writer who helped millions of people to dream big and achieve awesome results by becoming accountable to themselves and their organizations.

Accountability is not forced upon; rather it is a commitment that one freely makes to get the results that one wants. It takes care of both personal growth and organizational growth.

Does Ownership Include Control?

Most organizations are ruled by the managerial class! "Ownership means control. If there is no control then there is no ownership", says James Burnham, philosopher and political theorist.

"In every society there are two elites: those who have power and those who are attempting to seize it from the former group. These two are minorities and they do not represent the majority, the workers", he says. The former thinks they will get power if they have control. And if they have power they have ownership.

The best way to reach effectiveness is to eliminate ineffectiveness. This is possible only by understanding the true meaning of 'control'. "The purpose of control is not to control people but to control facts and information", says Mary Parker Follet, social scientist who challenged the precepts of scientific management and laid the foundations of the human relations school of management.

According to Follet, those organizations who invest in command and control will perish. The only viable form of control is coordination. Manager should become a coordinator or a facilitator.

"The machine bureaucracy demonstrated rigid hierarchical structures managed top down, controlling and limiting the creative energy of those below", says Chris Argyris, the proponent of Action Science. In machine bureaucracy, a manager manages by limiting others. He experiences a sense of ownership and fulfillment by controlling others.

> People are not cogs in machines. They have their own aspirations, goals, dreams and plans. Controlling them is not the role of the manager.

The digital world is shattering the machine bureaucracy. People are not cogs in machines. They have their own aspirations, goals, dreams and plans.

Controlling them is not the role of the manager. Controlling will not give ownership.

Do you wish to make your organization an ideal one? "Those at the top should give up their custodianship of knowledge and control. This means giving up their power so that they can empower others", says Max Boisot, who influenced the concept of Knowledge Management. The consequence, you gain more trust.

Ownership Breeds Trust

When you take ownership, your bosses will trust you and empower you. They will give you the resources and training required to succeed. They will stand by you when you fail and give you credit when you succeed. When you take up ownership of your job, your team too will trust you because you no longer believe in micromanagement or carrot and stick methods.

Trust is always at war with micromanagement.

Micromanagement is the enemy of ownership. Many leaders fall into a micromanagement mindset because either they are not capable of leading with a macro mindset or because they don't trust their team's ability to do things on their own. Instead we need to inspire them to become owners of their jobs. When we do this our team won't let us down.

Trust is in constant war with micromanagement. Leaders don't need to interfere in the work of the team unnecessarily. This gives them sufficient time to think about more significant, more prominent or more innovative things. Ownership breeds trust and trust in turn encourages ownership. It is a two-way process.

With an ownership mindset employees become frugal in the use of company resources. Wastages are reduced, money is saved, customers are retained and discipline is self-imposed. They make better decisions, become more motivated and discover valuable solutions to problems.

Communication is Crucial

Communication plays a vital role in building an ownership mindset. Communication has to be two-way. The employees should feel the confidence and freedom to talk transparently and express their ideas and opinions honestly. They will share great ideas in such an atmosphere.

When they work on their own ideas, ownership is the best. They take responsibility to solve their problems for they know their problems best. So organizations should give them the autonomy to try out various options and find a solution for themselves.

Don't play the blame game because the blame game gives birth to excuses. The owner takes not only the successes also the blames. He can't waste his time blaming others. He has to hunt for solutions and triumph over the crisis before competitors catch up. Instead of wasting time in blames, look for the best opportunity to learn new skills to improve performance.

How Devoted Are We?

I have elaborated extensively in my book, 'Salt and Light: A Leader or a Pilgrimage' that work is worship and our workplaces are places of worship. The question that comes up then is 'how devoted are we to our roles and responsibilities?' What is the degree of our fidelity to our work?

Devotion is no more a religious term. It has transcended to other areas of our lives too. Today we hear about devotion to parents, to spouse, to family, to work, to team etc. It is defined as a profound and passionate dedication to a person, a cause or an entity.

> Reading scriptures will not make us spiritual. Preaching about God is not going to make us holy. Instead if we live a life of values, with total devotion to our roles and responsibilities as a parent, spouse, child, colleague and employee then we become spiritual.

Religions teach us that devotion to God is superior to all other devotions. However, God himself, through his manifestations, shows us that the best devotion is to live a life worthy of one's calling and perform one's roles and responsibilities with utmost commitment.

Extreme longing for God is not spirituality. Reading scriptures will not make us spiritual. Renouncing the world or living an ascetic life is no guarantee to reach the Divine. Preaching about God is not going to make us holy.

Instead if we live a life of values, with total devotion to our roles and responsibilities as a parent, spouse, child, colleague and employee then we become spiritual.

It is said that a hand extended to lift up another is better than two hands folded in prayer. Thus if we become totally committed and devoted to our work, then we can humbly say that our work is our worship.

Work like an Intrapreneur

Many of us have read the story of Jonathan Livingston Seagull by Richard Bach. A thousand gulls daily fight for bits of food on the seashore. But one bird dares to be different and believes that the reason why he flies is not eating.

The rest of the birds confront Jonathan. "Why are you different, why can't you be like us?"

He is committed to his vision of flying high and is obsessed with the idea of pushing the limits of everything to discover a new world. His determination and commitment to his vision take him to a new world of perfection. He is excited to find in this new world birds like him.

Soon he remembers his brothers back on earth. So he decides to return to his community to train and coach other young birds who want to push themselves to reach higher existence of life. Jonathan tells his students, "We are unlimited ideas of freedom. Our whole body is nothing more than our thought."

Jonathan was an intrapreneur. Like him, we need to take ownership of our goals, dreams and works. Shall we take ownership of our life, peace and happiness? Shall we become an intrapreneur?

An intrapreneur takes ownership of his job and does it with passion and creativity within one's own company. We are entrepreneurs in our company.

Intrapreneurship is characterized by initiative, accountability, passion and creativity. Intrapreneurs are ambitious and result-driven; creative and innovative. They look for job satisfaction instead of job security. They are action-oriented with high energy and passionate self-starters. They reach immense heights but come back like Jonathan to uplift others. They take the risk to make a difference!

> There is no future in any job; the future lies in the one who holds the job.

An ownership mind finds its expression in varied ways like respecting and preserving the resources of the company, taking care of company property, appreciating the initiatives of coworkers, taking responsibility to solve problems, making things happen and following through from the start to the end.

They are ready to delegate, learn, accept blames, share credit, create a positive work culture and cherish an intrapreneurship spirit.

There is no future in any job; the future lies in the one who holds the job. We must be smarter than the people who hired us. We must exert ourselves and excel in whatever we do.

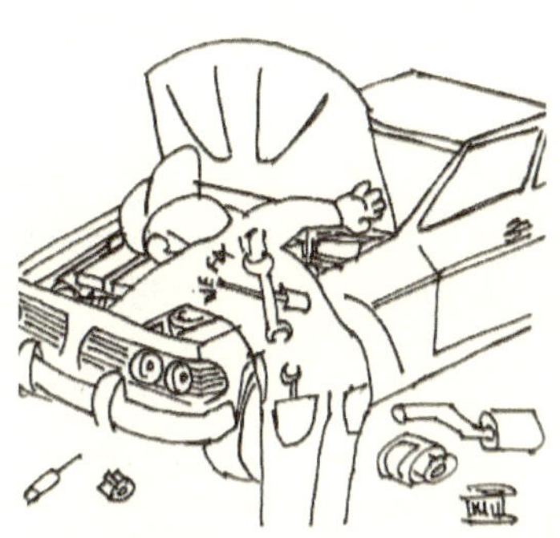

Dr. Samuel Johnson, the author of 'A Dictionary of English Language' once called upon his people and told them never to retire from work until the world feels sorry that they retired.

Work done grudgingly is servitude, work done willingly is service and work done lovingly is a sacrament.

Own your work and make it a sacrament. An ownership mind tells itself, "Hei, man, it's your job, own it".

The Light of Life

"Let us get up then;

Let us open our eyes to the Light.

It is time now for us to rise from sleep."

The Rule of St. Benedict

1

Eureka:
I Have Found It!

Hiero, the king of Syracuse who ruled Greece in the 3rd century BC, faced a peculiar problem. He believed the gods favoured him in the war against the Romans. As a gesture of thanksgiving to the gods, he wanted to offer a crown made of pure gold.

He gave the task to the best goldsmith in his country. The goldsmith, using the gold coins sanctioned by the king, made a crown and gave it to the king. The king was highly impressed with its beauty.

As he was going to the temple to offer it to the gods, he heard his ministers and servants whispering among themselves: "Our king is a fool! This goldsmith has cheated him. The crown is not pure gold."

The king became angry. He questioned the goldsmith. The goldsmith confirmed that he had used all the gold the king gave. However, the king had doubts but had no way to prove if the crown was an alloy or pure gold.

The king remembered his cousin Archimedes, an inventor of military equipment that helped him win many wars. He summoned Archimedes and presented the problem to him.

Archimedes did not know how to measure the purity of an irregular object like a crown. He did not know how to prove that the goldsmith had cheated the king and had mixed gold with an alloy of silver to make the crown.

That evening as he stepped into the bathtub filled with water, he noticed that as he put his legs into the bathtub, water gushed out. Thrilled, he removed his legs and tried again. Water flowed out again. Then as he slowly immersed himself inside the tub, he found more

water gushing out of the tub. Now he had a solution to the problem of the king.

Excited and happy, Archimedes ran out from the bathtub naked, running through the streets of Syracuse shouting 'Eureka', 'Eureka' which meant 'I have found it'. He had discovered a solution to the problem of the king.

Archimedes knew that though the mass of gold coins and crown might be the same because mass is the amount of matter in a solid which is not affected by gravity, their density would not be the same. Density is the quantity of matter per unit volume. "If I can measure the volume of the coins and the crown, I will be able to measure their densities", he thought.

For measuring the volume, he now had an idea. Just as the volume of the water dispersed by his body in the bathtub must be equal to the volume of his body submerged, he said he could measure the volume of the crown using the same principle. Volumes can indicate if the densities are the same or not.

As soon as he reached the palace, he asked the servants to bring two buckets filled with water. Then he immersed the gold coins in one bucket and the golden crown in the other. He found that the water displaced was not equal. This proved that the volumes were not the same. Since the volumes were not equal, he concluded that the goldsmith had indeed cheated the king. The goldsmith on interrogation admitted his crime and was punished for it.

Archimedes' 'Eureka' moment changed the history of the world. The principle of buoyancy born on that day is studied even today.

What about our Eureka moments?

There are so many Eureka moments in our life too. Unlike Archimedes, we have taken them for granted. We have forgotten to shout out 'Eureka' to celebrate those moments. There were times when we had been struggling to solve an issue and then from nowhere suddenly came a serendipity moment, a Eureka moment when we discovered a solution. All inventions were Eureka moments.

Identify your Eurekas; celebrate them.

Why are Ideas Important?

If we Google the websites of organizations, big or small, across the world, we find the word 'innovation' appearing many times on their pages. Everyone talks about it. Organizations, politicians, governments, public and private sectors, religious leaders and even families, schools and colleges speak about innovation. Everyone gets immersed in this word.

There are organizations that celebrate innovation days and innovation months, encouraging employees to participate in innovation related trainings, events and exhibitions. However just as no one gets drunk by thinking about the word wine, so too no one becomes innovative merely by talking about innovation.

Ideas are the investments we make to better our future. Some of us wonder why we should give ideas because our ideas rarely find implementation.

The ideas are like the seeds we plant. We plant it today but do not expect its fruits the next day. Though we don't see any developments on that seed, we know it's growing steadily to become a mighty tree.

Ideas create wealth both for the organization and for the employee. It ensures the organization's growth and employees' growth. They are able to bring out the best products and services for the customers and retain them for a lifetime. Ideas make our business competitive, get us recognized and thus we lead a life of fulfilment.

We face myriads of problems daily. We experience the pain. But a few of us discover opportunities amidst this pain. Everyone experiences problems and pains but only a few will use them as opportunities to innovate and find a solution to eradicate this pain. They discover the Eureka moments in their lives.

Creativity, Invention and Innovation

People often misunderstand these three terms. Creativity is defined as the 'generation of ideas.' It is the ideation process. Here our focus is to generate as many ideas as possible. It doesn't matter whether the ideas are feasible or not. What matters is the quantity of ideas not their quality.

When these ideas are put into action by developing a product, a process or a service, they are called inventions. When these inventions add value to organizations and society, they are called innovations. Value does not mean commercial values alone. It also means social values.

Every time we innovate, we need to ask ourselves how much value it is bringing to improve the lives of people. When an organization focuses on to improve the social value of its product or service, it also increases its financial value. Those leaders who solely focus on profit miss the opportunity to impact the market.

> Every time we innovate we need to ask ourselves how much value it is bringing to improve the lives of people.

Innovations Have a Social Value

Smartphones, for example, have tremendously impacted the society and connected the world together. The Printing Press helped to revolutionize the world for hundreds of years and enabled the world to benefit from it politically, socially and spiritually. If the innovation by the Wright Brothers brought the world closer, the innovations of pharmacy helped us to live longer and healthier.

All these have created value for the world and have given profits to the inventor.

Water scarcity has been causing much panic in the world in recent times. Pure drinking water is everyone's right. However many people in the world do not have access to this resource. Vestergaard Frandsen Company based in Switzerland invented a life-straw product that filters undrinkable water and makes it pure for people to drink. This innovation has saved many lives especially in Africa. These are innovations with a social value.

Think Out of the Box

The first step to become innovative is to learn tools that can help us to generate ideas. There are many idea generation tools which we can learn from experts, books or YouTube. However the basic quality required to become innovative is to 'think out of the box'.

We live comfortably in a world created by our upbringing, experience, education and values. All the rules, regulations and quality procedures ensure that we remain inside the box.

When we are inside the box, we deliver incremental changes and our bosses, organizations and customers are happy about that. However beyond a point, we fail to enjoy the Eureka moments as we are within the box.

Though we feel safe and secure within our boxes, our human dignity urges us to go out of the box. When we think out of the box, we risk our reputation which we carefully built over a period of time, we become disagreeable to those around and we face many uncertainties in life. As a result, we run back into our little safe boxes.

> 'Think out of the box' means to go beyond the limits of the mind, become unreasonable and challenge the existing practices to bring out a better solution to the problem.

Where is this box? What does it mean to 'go out of the box?'

The box is the boundary we have drawn in our minds based on our education, culture, upbringing, environment, experience, rules and regulations. However, the Eureka moments are beyond this box. The box prevents us from achieving the full potential.

'Think out of the box' thus means to go beyond the limits of the mind, become unreasonable and challenge the existing practices to bring out a better solution to the problem.

Organizations like Google, 3M and Hyundai encourage employees to think out of the box. Hyundai, for example, includes in its management philosophy the concept of 'continually challenging the new frontiers.' The frontiers are the borders formulated by the human mind.

We might have a bright idea. Immediately our mind dictates borders like: 'it's already done', 'it won't be accepted by the management or by the customers', 'there is no budget', 'it won't work'. As a result, we give up those beautiful ideas and run back into the luxury of our little boxes.

We all know that shipping containers are used to ferry goods from one place to another. In 1956, an inventor by name Philip C. Clarke decided to think out of the box. He converted these old steel containers into restaurants and habitable buildings and offices. I have seen in many manufacturing companies these containers today used as offices and canteens for their staff.

Tools like Mind Mapping, invented by Tony Buzan, a renowned author and educationalist or Brain Storming or Scamper are excellent methods to generate ideas. We need to learn more about these tools if we are hungry for idea generation tools.

While generating ideas, we must remember the following things. In any idea generation exercise quantity is more important than quality. We should also never judge an idea. Who are we to say whether an idea is good or bad?

The ideas thought to be bullshit once transformed the world totally at a later stage. So we must resist our temptation to praise one idea or condemn another. "A mediocre idea that generates enthusiasm can go further than a great idea that inspires no one", says Mary Kay Ash, the founder of Mary Kay Cosmetics. Hence all ideas are great ideas.

Roadblocks to Innovation

We all appreciate the importance of innovation and we agree 'it's a part of human dignity to innovate'. But have we ever realized that we act as roadblocks to bring out our own innovative ideas and crush down the ideas of other people?

While strong hierarchical and dismissive cultures prevalent in many organizations have killed many ideas, it's our own experience that has been the biggest murderer of ideas.

"This is a stupid and silly idea. We have tried it many times and it won't work in the current circumstances." How often have we heard these words from our seniors? This is a clear example of a dismissive culture. They view new ideas as time wasters.

When the world was moving towards computerization Thomas Watson, Chairman, IBM said in 1943, "I think there is a world market for maybe five computers." The Western Union wrote off the telephone in 1876, saying, "This telephone has too many shortcomings to be seriously considered as a means of communication." These kinds of organizational roadblocks to innovation are there everywhere, every time.

Every now and then I encounter people in my trainings who say, "My boss stole my ideas and he got the appreciation from the management." These credit grabbers destroy the culture of innovation in an organization. When we remove these roadblocks, ideas will flow like a river.

Our Experience: the Biggest Roadblock

Have you ever recognized that your experience, education and upbringing are the biggest roadblocks to innovation? Recently while I organized an idea generation contest, I found that most of the senior employees didn't show much interest, while the new joiners and millennials were very active participants.

The veterans with a richer experience and higher levels of knowledge were more unwilling to share their ideas than the youngsters. No wonder today many organizations hurry to campuses to hire with a view to bring fresh ideas and new thinking into the system.

A closer look at this phenomena made me realize that the seniors were not unwilling to share their ideas. It was more because of the fear of taking the risk of sharing an idea that they declined to share. When you share an idea, your idea will be judged since it's a contest. So the fear of losing the contest against the juniors prevented them from sharing ideas.

Another reason I found was that the seniors were more cautious while the youngsters were more spontaneous. Since they were cautious, they wanted to spend more time on information collection, on analysis and wanted to take time to test the ideas before they presented them to the management.

With their experience, they knew there could be possibly many solutions. So they required time to discover more solutions and select the best. It was a tedious process and so decided to give up.

It is important that the senior employees learn to defeat their fears, nurture their innovative attitude and come out of their comfort zones to become more innovative at work.

The Dopamine Effect

Archimedes had his Eureka moment while he was in a bathtub. Like many of you, I too have had many innovative and wonderful ideas while in the bathroom which have helped me to make my programs more impactful!

Everyone has similar experiences. We suddenly get an excellent idea, when we are relaxed, during a morning walk, while reading, watching a film, driving, praying, while in the bath or even when doing nothing.

Dopamine is the molecule that motivates us to act and respond to situations in a pleasurable way. When we experience this pleasure, we repeat that action.

Some years ago, there was an ideation contest in our organization. I had never participated in such events earlier. A young colleague of mine participated and shared its screenshot with the rest of us in the team. This motivated me to participate.

I gave one idea, was so excited by the act that I gave the second and then the third and it went on and on till I reached ten ideas. I still had more ideas to share. I was enjoying the effect of dopamine and experienced the thrill of generating so many ideas in such a short time.

This is the power of dopamine on our brain cells. The more you share, the more you will experience the pleasure of sharing.

I had a pleasant surprise when one of my ideas was selected as the best idea from among 10,000 ideas! I received a cash prize and a certificate from the MD. Look at the effect of dopamine!

There are No Full Stops!

"We need to remember that there are no full stops in innovation, but only commas. Nothing in life is final", says Dr. N. Annamalai who has done extensive research on innovation and is an eminent faculty of Creativity and Innovation.

Our world longs to become better every day. We shouldn't assume that the solution we have today is the final solution. There can be a better solution tomorrow.

"The questions we face in life are mostly open-ended. 95% of the questions are open-ended. But we live in the 5% realm and are happy with these close-ended questions", says Dr. Annamalai.

> The moment we put a full stop in life we die. Instead learn to use more commas and live on to generate more ideas.

What is alarming is that our schools and colleges teach us to give answers to this 5% of questions only. They never inspire us to become innovative.

Before we use a full stop, it's good to use a comma and ask 'what else.' This will give us more options to decide. The more 'what else' we use, the more ideas we discover.

The moment we put a full stop in life we die. Instead learn to use more commas and live on to generate more ideas.

How to Become Innovative?

When the participants of my trainings ask me to teach them to become more innovative I suggest the following simple tips.

1. Include Ideation in Your To-Do List

While you prepare your 'to-do list' for the day, assign 15 minutes daily for innovative thinking. The employees of 3M follow a 15 % rule. They spent 15% of their time daily to pursue innovative ideas. Decide that within these 15 minutes, you will give two new ideas.

It can be on any topic not necessarily related to work. You can even look at things like celebrating your parents wedding anniversary or going out for a picnic with your colleagues. This exercise will help you to develop the habit of idea generation.

2. Prefer Quantity to Quality

Instead of one solution, think of 10 solutions. Remember in ideation quantity is more important than quality.

When you give one idea, dopamine begins its work on your brain and you discover more ideas and more Eureka moments. This is how I won the ideation contest. Enjoy the dopamine effect and go on giving large quantity of ideas without evaluating its quality.

3. Always Ask: 'What Else'

This is the secret to transform the world. Always use open-ended questions in ideation. Full stops will kill creativity. 'What else' will give you new perspectives on existing problems and will give you numerous solutions. Make it a practice to use 'what else' in your conversations.

I suggest this simple technique to parents when they come to me for counseling. Children develop their lateral and intuitive thinking skills and nurture a sense of wonder when adults use 'what else' in their conversations with them.

4. Improve Your Knowledge

We can share only if we have something. We should continuously update ourselves by reading, studying and attending trainings on innovation. When we expose ourselves to new ideas, new knowledge and new experiences we think with a new perspective.

Look out for opportunities to improve every day. Make sure to learn something new daily.

5. Move from 'I wish I Can' to 'How I Can'

We all wish to make a change in the world. While we sit and wish, others take action and change the world. Instead of wishes, look at actions.

If you want to buy an Alcazar, instead of sitting and wishing, chart out a plan to own that beautiful car.

Eureka moments are not the privileges of a few. Archimedes experienced it. It's there in abundance for us too.

We need to think out of the box to discover the opportunities and ensure those ideas have social values.

It is said that the best ideas are found in cemeteries. Those were people with excellent ideas which were never shared and implemented. Let us not take our ideas to the graves!

2

The Corporate Monks

Benedict of Nursia, the saintly monk who lived in Italy, founded Monte Cassino, a community for monks, in Rome in 529 AD. As the father of western monasticism, he formulated a set of rules called the Rule of Life. It has left its reverberations on education, politics, social, religious and spiritual dimensions of our lives. These rules were futuristic, balanced, moderate and humane. It dealt with matters related to both secular and sacred.

The rules had a profound influence on the emergence of western civilization, culture and values. His philosophical thoughts lighted the dark nights of European history and paved the way for enlightenment.

The teachings and thoughts of Benedict have influenced many Governments and their constitutions across the world. He was a lantern that illuminated the world and inspired his followers to do the same.

What does it mean to illuminate the world? What does it mean to be a corporate hermit?

Hope Illuminates

A hermit is a person of hope. Hope tells us to believe in the light that is present at the other side of the darkest phase of our life. The corporate hermits live by this optimism.

Benedict believed in people and filled them with hope. He knew people had immense potential and they could achieve marvellous things if given the right opportunities and training. Those who live with hope take risks, fail at times, and always learn from failures.

Hope tells us to reward not the successes alone but the failures too. Nelson, a friend of our family, invited my wife and me for a party recently. He was celebrating the result of his son. The boy had passed his secondary school exams with 45% marks! Parents of this courage are rare!

There is an inner war in everyone. Humans will err. Punishment will not give cure to these indulgences, injuries and impulses. Some may misuse or abuse these allowances at times.

If one wishes to be a corporate hermit, one must live by this hope, learn from failures and should make earnest efforts to overcome one's weaknesses.

Are we living with hope? Can we give hope to those who have lost it? Can we illuminate our teams, societies and homes? If we do so, we are hermits!

Knowledge Enlightens

Just as Benedict was a great believer in the power of education, every corporate hermit is a champion of learning and development in his organization. He assigned time for daily study and teaching. He realized that only an enlightened mind could lead the world.

Intense training was given to those who lacked knowledge and skills. Every trainee was personally coached and mentored to become an expert in his area of interest. He introduced the coaching system in his monastery and made the seniors responsible for developing their juniors.

He was a practitioner and believed in translating learning into action. Every learner has to implement what he learns in life, at work

> Every learner has to implement what he learns in life, at work or in his interpersonal relationships.

or in his interpersonal relationships. Similarly every corporate monk should foster a learning culture in his team.

During the one-on-one coaching, the disciple of Benedict had to narrate the fruits of the learning they tasted and the struggles they experienced while implementing the learning. The coaches then would guide and correct their paths.

Benedict used his rhetorical skills to inspire innovation in people. Just as a hammer is used to build a house or to destroy it, learning can help people to become virtuous, committed and spiritual, provided it is made actionable.

The education philosophy of Benedict played a major role in the reclamation and regeneration of Europe. It aimed at the physical, intellectual, social, moral and spiritual upliftment of students. Similarly, our corporate education should go beyond the workplace and should become holistic. It should enlighten the learner.

Education can form and reform a society. While most of the politicians use rhetoric to covet power, Benedict used it to transform societies. A lot of executives waste a lot of their time on gossip or on pretty issues. Lunch, dinners and even meetings become avenues to spread their negativism and unjust criticisms.

Negativity is evil. So, Benedict innovated 'Lectio Divina', the practice of reading spiritual books during meals. A person was assigned the task of reading while others listened and ate. This helped in fostering positivity in his organization.

Organizations invest a lot in employee development. Are these investments giving results and contributing to the success of the organization? This is a critical question to be answered by everyone. Training should not be for a good feeling. It should nurture business and should result in ROI. It should aim at the holistic development of people.

HR: Hard Rules or Heart Rules?

Stress, depression, breakups and struggles are part of professional life. Work from home, hybrid workplaces and remote monitoring have aggravated this to a great extent. In this context, it is important that we treat each other well. Rules and regulations, policies and processes, structures and systems have to become humane and motherly.

A few months ago I participated in a HR Conference in Chennai as a keynote speaker. After the session, a young participant told me that HR often talks about hard rules devoid of empathy. Human Resources has put on the vest of policies, rules and regulations. HR and HR professionals represent rules and policies.

A mature organization requires rules, policies and regulations. But organizations require professionals who will treasure the person not the policy at their hearts. Policies, structures, systems and rules must foster a balance of work and life. Our HR policies should become inspirational not just informational.

The Rules of Benedict ensured good food, safe shelter, modest dress, healthy sleep, dignified work and sufficient recreation for everyone. He introduced the three-shift pattern, assigned six hours each for manual labour and spiritual work and allotted four hours for self-study and research. Eight hours were kept aside for sleep.

The happy are those who lead a balanced life. Moderation is the key to happiness. It helps to lead a dignified life. Everyone needs work, food, shelter, rest, study and sleep. If anyone of these is exaggerated the wheel of life becomes flat and stops to move forward.

The Spirituality of Work

'Salt and Light' has elaborated in depth on the power of work in sanctifying oneself. Every work and every worker is noble. Work is the surest path to enlightenment. It is a good activity for healthy and joyful living. Imagine of a life in plenty but you have nothing to do. What a disastrous life it will be?

Grace and divinity don't dwell in an idle heart.

It doesn't matter what we do, for every work is noble. So whether I am a cook or a carpenter, a painter or a professor, a doctor or a farmer, a sweeper or a scientist, a musician or a mason, what makes me noble is my intension with which I work.

Human beings are created to work and should engage in work. Work is the only way to partake in the creative action of God. Benedict frowned on idleness and laziness and rewarded commitment and hard work.

Grace and divinity don't dwell in an idle heart. Hence he proposed the spirituality of 'ora et labora', 'prayer and work', paving the way for a new spirituality of work. A life of fulfilment embraces both spiritual and temporal life. "One does not live by bread alone; but by every word that comes from the mouth of God", says Jesus Christ.

Hermits are not those who run off to the mountains or to the deserts to live in solitude. Instead they live among their followers sowing the seeds of love, forgiveness and hope rather than fear, hatred and frustration. In such organization, people will perform their roles, even manual labour with new dignity and pride.

Fairness, Equality and Equity

Though societies and organizations are predominantly hierarchical respect, rewards and punishments should be fair. Leaders should treat everyone with fairness and equality.

Benedict championed the concept of equity in addition to equality and fairness. Equality, yes; but equity is more vital for any organization.

He allowed differential and equitable treatments based on age, capabilities, health, physical conditions, basic needs and spiritual mastery. Equality is not the answer to the problems of the world. The world needs the ointment of equity to heal the wounds caused by historically accepted social injustices. There are people who deserve a preferential treatment.

Fairness, equality and equity are to be practised in daily life and in the ordinary conversations of everyone. "Keep your tongue free from vicious talk and your lips from all deceit; turn away from evil and do good; let peace be your quest and aim", says the Rule.

The Light of Innovation and Entrepreneurship

Every hermit is an innovator and an entrepreneur. When monks led wandering lives and lived in solitude, Benedict innovated and introduced the concept of community living. Human beings are created to live in community. Living and working together, guided by a set of rules will help everyone to unleash his or her immense potential to reach enlightenment.

Many philosophers attracted their disciples with the teaching that happiness was the fruit of conquering wealth, success, status, knowledge and fame. Aristotle, for example, proposed that only such lives were noble. Through his innovative and entrepreneurial acts, Benedict contradicted these thoughts. He was a startup founder who proposed that the path to happiness and enlightenment was by living in a community and leading a life of brotherhood.

Modern families are getting divided, distanced and disillusioned for no reason. The earning abilities of couples give them independence and they decide to walk on different paths even in the slightest pain.

We have lost the sense of divinity in marriages and are unable to experience the power of sacrifices and sacredness in family life. We are losing fast the element of wonder in relationships.

People stay under the same roof separated by substantial emotional distances. They have nothing much in common. They have no time for a family meal or for an outing. Each one lives his or her life glued to gadgets. If we don't re-establish the sacredness of marriage we are doomed to live in horror.

Business organizations are not different from families. Both are communities of commitment. Though working from home became essential during the pandemic, organizations that believe in brotherhood communities are rushing back to workplaces as they have experienced the immense benefits of working together. Benedict's invention of workplace as a forum to collaborate and create synergy is still relevant even after hundreds of years.

A coenobitic life lived in a community is more beneficial than an eremitic life where one lives in solitude, cut off from one's brothers and sisters. Human life is communitarian. We are what we are because of our relationships with others.

> A coenobitic life lived in community is more beneficial than an eremitic life where one lives in solitude cut off from one's brothers and sisters.

Every organization should reverberate with values of kindness, compassion, forgiveness, care, concern, charity and humility. People are the best assets. Yes;

often on papers and policies of HR. An effective HR ensures that these get reflected in the daily life of everyone.

Just as Benedict visualized what his followers and customers required and went out of the way to delight them we too are to identify ways to strengthen our commitment to our internal and external customers.

He innovated a social movement that is relevant even today. He identified a propitious niche for his ideas and customized them to the right market fit. He asked the right questions like a good entrepreneur to give the best solutions. He innovated to make the world brighter. The corporate monks' mandates are the same.

The Brotherhood Organizations

The rules of Benedict were democratic and were meant for self-governing and autonomous communities. It helped them to foster brotherhood and strong affection for each other. Manufacturing and hospitality organizations, for example, foster brotherhood teams. Though the strong affection for each other is distorted by trends like work from home and working in remote, many organizations are returning to the spirit of brotherhood.

Geographical isolation, social and emotional distancing and remote monitoring work styles are causing much havoc to teams and their performance. They contribute to inefficiency and make the team immobile in moving towards customer delight. As a result, potential customers are lost and markets get vanished.

Benedict innovated the idea of democratic functioning of teams. Many Governments liked this idea and drafted their constitutions based on these rules. It acted as a catalyst in advocating the cause of workers and paved the way for the concept of dignified labour during the industrial revolution. The believers of democratic teams are reaping the harvests unlike the non-believers.

The Benedictine monks have been great influencers in the world for the last 1500 years. They remained relevant in their commitment to society. The world prospered because of them, but they remained unaffected by this prosperity. They were immune to the valueless world and when political leaders became a threat to democracy they opposed them with revolutionary ideas and strict personal disciplines.

The Spirituality of Hospitality

Kengeri is a small town on Bangalore Mysore highway. As a student of Theology in the late '90s my batch had the opportunity to stay at the Benedictine monastery at Kengeri as part of our curriculum.

We learnt much from those eminent men who were once professional engineers, professors and scientists who chose to lead a life in the monastery in deep humility doing manual labour like taking care of the farm, the animals and spending their time in prayer, writing and study.

I was fascinated by the idea that inspired them to give up worldly lives and live enclosed within the walls with no contact with the outside world. We were not allowed to go beyond certain permitted areas of the monastery. We felt a lot of mystery beyond the doors. We could hear the chanting of hymns every now and

then which would break the deep silence that enveloped the cloister.

In spite of all hardships and severe lifestyles that they embraced, everyone looked serene, happy, peaceful and amazingly charming!

Our world of divisions, disunity and disharmony is getting cured and transformed by virtuous lives of such men and women.

I enjoyed their hospitality, kindness and immense positive spirits. They served us with luxury while they lived in poverty. They ensured we had a great time while they lived deprived of basic needs. Later in life, I curated a training on Service Excellence based on the experience I had at the monastery.

They don't perform a set of KPIs. They don't do anything for rewards, merits or promotions. They just spread the light, laughter and love like the tiny fireflies.

They possess nothing yet they give everything: care, compassion, consideration and confidence to everyone including strangers and even enemies. They endure hardships to ensure good times for others.

As executives we are invited to create the same magical moments for those who come to us. Service is the future; not products or sales. As a result, organizations are vying to differentiate themselves based on their service. This differentiation is the result of the human factor.

The Darkness of Pretension

We pretend a lot and thus bring darkness into lives. We pretend to be what we are not at work, at home, in relationships and in every area of our lives. Our masks hide our real selves. We have ignored our real selves and projected a false self with the intention to be accepted and liked by everyone.

We need to reroute our behaviours in a socially acceptable manner. But this doesn't mean that we sacrifice our real selves. Pretention prevents the light from entering the hearts.

> When we remove the vest of pretension we become respectable, compassionate and humble.

Can I live without pretension? Am I ready to fail and accept its responsibility? Am I willing to accept my shortcomings? Am I ready to exhibit my real self? Am I living an authentic life, true to what I am and what I think?

Pretensions make us morally corrupt. It forces us to live somebody's life. It makes us lose our identity and we choose to live somebody's life. In-authentic and non-transparent people, especially at the leadership roles ruin the culture, values and life. They propagate darkness.

When we remove the vest of pretension, we become respectable, compassionate and humble. Thus we find a deep sense of purpose in life.

Obedience to superior and organizational policies is still a virtuous act! Fidelity is still sacred in life. Faithfulness is our response to what we are asked or entrusted with. Doing what we are entrusted with full commitment and truthfulness is faithfulness.

When a task is done with total devotion to it and for the benefit of the customers and not to please a boss or to gain good rewards, we are faithful to the work that is entrusted to us.

The Hard Choices a Hermit Makes

Benedict was born in a noble family. As a young child, he was sent to Rome to study rhetoric and philosophy. He excelled in public speaking with amazing rhythm, conviction and eloquent skills to influence his listeners.

He had everything a youth of those days would long for: wealth, health, education and aristocratic background. Unfortunately, such youths often pursued a life of pleasure and lived in darkness.

He chose a different path, the un-trodden path. The path of truth and light.

He viewed Rome as a sin city. He knew living in Rome would ruin his life. So he fled Rome and its seductive charms. He gave up his noble status, his wealthy inheritance and his worldly friends. He ran away to a cave on top of a mountain called the Monte Cassino and stayed there for the rest of his life in solitude and contemplation.

He chose to become a hermit!

Life wasn't easy as a hermit. A desire for pretty women, luxurious lifestyles and thirst for power often tempted him. Initially, he would resist these temptations by punishing himself. Gradually he gained mastery over his impulses, indulgences and imperfections by strenuous self-control, self-denial and self-mortification. Determination defeated the power of desires.

When his fame began to spread, followers multiplied. He didn't want to be their leader. He wanted to be their servant. He advocated the example of Jesus Christ who was a servant leader.

He told the people that he would be extremely strict and disciplined if they chose him their leader. They insisted. But when they realized he meant what he said, they tried to throw him out and even poisoned him a few times. He survived the attempts on his life.

Are we willing to pursue what our heart desires? Are we ready to give up the excess desire for wealth, status and power though they are our legitimate rights? Are we ready to become a servant? Can we face suffering and humiliation? How do we respond to self-sacrifice, self-control and acts of mortification?

Are we ready to follow the path of a hermit?

Every corporate hermit has to make hard choices. They live among the crowd and not in the cave. They live in communities of commitment at the workplaces and not in solitude on the mountains. They are detached from the vices but not from humanity. They live among us. They give their best to impact the world positively.

They live in peace, tranquility, light and love.

<table><tr><td>**3**</td><td></td></tr></table>

Are You Ready for the Risk?

L ife is beautiful because of the risks it embraces. Every risk involves some kind of uncertainty and potential dangers that might arise out of unknown causes. Nothing much in life is certain.

We experience some amount of insecurity even when we live a life of abundance. Every relationship has some risks in it. Risks are there in family, in business, in friendship and in all areas of life.

Risk is like the Damocles Sword

There is a 'Damocles sword' in every risk. Damocles was a general in the palace of Dionysius, the king of Sicily. He always felt jealous of the lavish and magnificent lifestyle of the king. "How happy I would be if I had all these wealth and power, even for a day", he wished.

> Life is beautiful because of the risks it embraces.

When Dionysius heard about the greed of Damocles, he offered to make him king for a day so that he could enjoy the rights and privileges of a king. Damocles was extremely delighted with the proposal that he readily accepted it. He enjoyed the power that was bestowed on him for a day. He feasted by eating, drinking and having fun the whole day.

Late that evening, fully drunk with pride and happiness, he looked up and found that there was a sharp sword hung by a single hair of a horse above his throne. At that moment, fear took over his greed. Damocles realized what it was to be a king. It was not just feasting and eating alone; it was a huge risk and a big responsibility.

Though he had much privileges and a lot of men and women waiting on him, he also had a sword hanging above his head. Realizing the risks involved, he begged the king to forgive him and give him back his original role.

This story reminds us that success is not the outcome of luck. Success will not come without effort. Our success is proportionate to the risks we take in life. One quality that all successful people have demonstrated down through the ages is that they are willing to embrace risks.

As we said, risks are there in every role and more so in greater responsibilities. Life is not worth living without risks either. The lives of all successful people tell these dazzling stories of risks they have taken. "It's not the mountain that we conquered today, it's ourselves", said

Edmund Hilary of New Zealand as he conquered Everest along with Tenzing Norgay of Nepal on May 29, 1953.

They didn't reach the tallest summit of about 29,035 feet above sea level just like that. They faced repeated failures, struggles and risks. The cruising altitude, low oxygen levels, freezing climate, dangerous avalanche and stormy weather had killed many already and some had even totally vanished on their journey.

The Everest, however, could not kill the unremitting spirit of humans. Despite the risks involved people, even today, continue to enjoy the thrill of defeating the tallest mountain in the world. They exemplify the risk-taking attitude of people.

Why Risk?

When life can be safe and secure, why should we risk our wealth, career and reputation? Some of us like to

live in status quo, while the brave will take calculated risks and achieve exponential success in life. "The biggest risk is not taking any risk. In a fast-changing world, the only strategy guaranteed to fail is not taking risks", says Mark Zuckerberg, the founder of Facebook.

Henry Ford took the risk of democratizing automobiles. When he was nowhere in the picture of auto companies, he put for himself an audacious goal to become the best automaker in the world.

He slashed the prices so that common man could afford a car. He took the risk of increasing production by introducing an assembly line in his shop floor. He reduced the working time of his employees and improved their packages to motivate them to work harder and better. He worked hard, slept less and took more risks till he achieved his goals.

Harry Potter and its legendary author J.K. Rowling, before they became hit makers, were huge risks for the publishers. She had a story that she thought could help people to fantasize. But her struggle to find a publisher failed many times.

As a single mother, living on a meagre welfare, rejected and ridiculed by all, she lived a life full of risks. She always wanted to be a storyteller. Her parents discouraged the idea. She was born in a poor family and her mother died of cancer. She did part-time job, stayed in a small room and would visit the cafes to sit and write her story.

At times she became severely depressed and even thought of ending her life. It was then that she channelized her energy and remained focused to complete her book. These risks could not kill her spirits.

When she completed her book in 1995, she, with much excitement, sent it to different publishers only to face rejection. She was ready to wait and continued to take risks. Finally Bloomsbury Publishing decided to publish her story in 1997 and she became an overnight celebrity.

In 1998 her book was made into a film by Warner Bros. The film became one of the super hits and collected $ 1 billion and she spent most of her money on philanthropy. The risks that she took transformed her life from rags to riches.

Elon Musk is another immense source of inspiration for everyone when we think of the benefits of taking risks. He made a fortune from PayPal that he had co-founded. Instead of launching a company similar to PayPal, he risked his fortune to launch Tesla Motors and SpaceX.

In the years that followed, he continued to invest in these two organizations that were not making any profits. His critics were too harsh on his decisions and his companies almost collapsed. However, he didn't give up. He was optimistic about the risk that he had taken. Today both Tesla and SpaceX are leading the world to the future.

All these risk-takers teach us the lesson that risks push us out of our comfort zones. We all take so many risks in life. "No pain, no gain" says the adage. In the same way, 'no risk, no reward'!

> Risks push us out of our comfort zones. No pain, no gain. No risk, no reward!

Elamparithi, my colleague in my previous organization, was a fantastic and high potential talent with a great future. After ten years of prosperous career, he decided to move on. He surprised everyone when he decided to join his uncle's startup. At our organization, he had a steady income. Joining a startup meant huge risks. But he was ready for the risk.

As he began to taste success, he launched a food product distribution company on his own. He didn't stop there either. He created a new brand of restaurant called 'Ponni's Marutham' and is hoping to launch more branches of his restaurant in different parts of Tamil Nadu.

The Parable of Risk

You take risks when you fall in love and when you get married. You take risks when you decide to have your family or change your job. When you start your car, aren't you taking a risk? Life is a travel from one risk to another.

The Parable of Talent that we discussed in a previous chapter is also called as the Parable of Risk. The master took the risk of giving his money to his servants. The servants were expected to invest the money wisely and get it multiplied.

The first two servants took the risk of investing their talents and doubled their income, while the third servant was afraid of taking risks that he hid the talent until the master returned.

The master punished the servant for not taking risks. Probably the master would have been happy if he had invested the amount and would have forgiven him even if he had incurred losses. Unwillingness to take risks from the side of the servant causes much anger in the master. It is better to take a risk and fail than not to take risks.

Many organizations encourage their employees to take risks. I have been fortunate to work under some of the best leaders who would encourage us to take risks irrespective of the outcomes. We were never punished for taking risks or for failing. We were punished for not taking risks and hiding our talents when the organization required us to move on.

AV Joseph, my schoolmate who runs a highly successful auto parts dealership once confided to me that the growth was the result of the many risks he had taken in life. He had a lucrative job in Delhi. He gave up the comfort of a steady income to launch a startup. Friends and relatives warned him. Critics scoffed. But he was ready for the jump, into the unknown.

Like the third servant, we can always meet people who shirk the opportunity to take risks. They sit and watch while others progress in life.

There are three kinds of people in the world: those who make things happen, those who watch things happen and those who wonder what happened. People like Joseph decided to make things happen.

To which group do we belong?

Risk is Action Oriented

Risk involves action. Thinking about risk and doing nothing is not risk. If the result is good, we celebrate;

if it's not, we learn from it and improve the next time. However not taking action is the tragedy in life and we will be punished for it just as it happened in the parable of the risk.

The important thing in life is our willingness to try before we give up. "It is common sense to take a risk and try it. If it fails, admit it frankly. But try something", says Franklin D. Roosevelt. Failing to try because of fear is one of our biggest challenges.

> Not taking risk should be a punishable act.

Taking risk also involves taking responsibility for the outcomes. We can't blame others for our failed attempts. The 3rd servant blamed the master for not investing his money. No one wants a blamer. Everyone seeks a doer.

We blame the Government for the increase in corruption, crimes and for the deterioration of values, harmony and peace in the world. We blame the bosses, the organizations, the politicians, the systems, the parents and the teachers. We blame everyone in the world.

Instead of blaming, can we take the responsibility to fix something to make this world better? This is the action we need to take today. "It is better to light a small candle than to curse the darkness", says Eleanor Roosevelt.

Light your lantern and help others to light theirs.

A Risk Taker or a Security Seeker?

Risks can both excite and scare people. Some people love risks while others love status quo. Though risk is associated with every sphere of life, most of us rely on security and love to play it safe.

Risks may appear to be dangerous. But often it's not so. Vikram, my friend, is an accomplished professor at a reputed engineering college. He is also an accomplished researcher who has many patents to his credit. Yet he repeatedly declines the offers he gets to represent his institution at international forums. When we asked him why he did so, he replied that he was scared of travelling by flight.

People think it's less risky to travel by car than by rail or plane. However statistics reveal that it is much less hazardous to travel by air than by car. Airplanes are 75 times safer than cars! We hear of fatal road accidents daily while we hear about air crashes very rarely. Yet people like Vikram are afraid to take the risk of flying.

Winners look at risk as an opportunity to experiment and succeed. They focus on the potential success and not on the failures. They are ready to face the punishments if they fail.

> When we don't take any responsibility we accomplish nothing in life.

This power of optimism along with their enterprising and never say die attitude take them through to discover success at the end. They take charge of the situation and prepare themselves instead of trusting in divine help and luck.

Since they can visualize success, they prepare themselves accordingly and grab the opportunities as they come by. When this happens the losers will call it luck while the winners will call it risk.

Risk Includes Responsibility

"A person can give up anything except his responsibility", says John C. Maxwell, the renowned leadership coach and author. Lord Krishna urged the Pandavas who were known to be gamblers to take the risk and enter into battle to regain their throne and royalty which rightly belonged to them.

Arjuna and the team are besieged with doubt and guilt for having to fight against their cousins. "Of the gamblers I am the risk, and of the noble I am their efficacy", says Lord Krishna. They were noble souls. Hence Krishna reminds them to take the responsibility involved in the risk and become victorious.

Risk involves responsibility and action. Doubt, seeking security and living in anxiety are the results of non-action. When we don't take any responsibility, we accomplish nothing in life. This leads to more self-doubt and self-negation. So Krishna asks the Pandavas to take the risk and get into the battlefield.

We may bleed, lose some resources, may be called unreasonable and unconventional. But ultimately, victory rests with those who take risk.

Taking risk is not gambling. People take lotteries and wait for the lady luck to hug them. This is not risk.

Risk involves calculated steps based on proper study and analysis of the situation. We need to study the background of the risk, compare it with other options, identify potential risks that might emerge in addition to the current risk, evaluate them, take action and take responsibility for the outcomes.

Risks which are beyond our capabilities and not based on our resources are difficult to achieve and chasing them will be more like gambling. Gambling is for those who trust in luck. But we trust in calculated risks.

Those who take risks set big goals and they do not believe in incremental improvements. They are champions of transformation. Those who remain at status quo or those who look for mediocre results are ordinary achievers while those who take calculated risks enjoy benefits beyond their imaginations. No one achieved anything big in life by playing safe.

We may bleed, lose some resources, may be called unreasonable and unconventional. But ultimately, victory rests with those who take risk.

When you take risks, you also take up the responsibility to reskill and up-skill yourself to meet the challenges that will emerge on your way. Soon you realize that you are beyond the chains of limiting beliefs that held you enslaved in the past.

When you go beyond your limiting beliefs you begin to believe in yourself and in the people around you. They become co-creators of your dream. The whole process becomes exciting and energizing and it doesn't matter to you even if you fail to reach your goals because you have enjoyed the process itself.

One of the biggest tragedies in human history happened on 15th April 1912. The largest, most sophisticated and most luxurious Titanic sank on that fateful night in the Atlantic Ocean.

Titanic was on its maiden voyage from Great Briton to New York carrying nearly 2500 people. The iceberg killed more than 1500 people. Indeed this was one of the most painful tragedies that the world experienced.

However the real tragedy was something else!

There were three other ships near Titanic as it sank. One of them was Sampson. It was just 7 miles away from Titanic and they saw the white flares signaling danger emerging from Titanic begging for help. But the crew of Sampson had been hunting seals illegally and they didn't want to be caught. So they steered their ship away and went in the opposite direction, away from Titanic.

How often do we avoid taking risks and continue with the status quo?

How often we too fail to take responsibility, fail to perform our obligations and seek safety and security? Taking risk is troublesome. Like these crew we too run away from risks so often and pretend as if we have not seen the impending danger.

The second ship was called Californian. It was 14 miles away from Titanic and was surrounded by icebergs. The Captain of the ship looked out and saw the white flares but since the conditions were not favorable and since it was night, he decided to go back to bed and wait until morning.

How often are we like these crew who though can do something, still won't do it because we are unwilling to risk and lament over the issue saying, 'what can I do' and we wait for right conditions to do something?

Another ship by name Carpathia was about 58 miles away from Titanic when they heard about the shipwreck from a radio. The Captain of the ship knelt down, prayed to God for courage, skill, wisdom and goodness and then steered the ship around and went straight ahead through the ice field to save 705 survivors of Titanic.

These were the real heroes who risked their lives. They demonstrated that what makes humans is not knowledge or skills but wisdom and goodness.

Today employers are looking for candidates with strong risk taking aptitude. The skills and knowledge that gave us pride and fame are fast sinking in the ocean of rapid changes. We need to hone new skills and develop risk-taking attitude to swim through the evolving world.

"You cannot discover new oceans unless you have the courage to lose sight of the shore", says Roy B. Zuck in The Speaker's Quote Book. People with a risk-taking mindset have a better chance to thrive on and reach the shore.

4 Light Your Lantern

anterns occupy a sacred place in every religion. For some people, it represents divinity; for others, it lights their paths. Some cultures believe that the lanterns lead the souls of the dead to eternal life or heavenly bliss.

The Chinese believe that on the eve of the New Year festival, the souls of their ancestors visit their families. In order to welcome these ancestors, they decorate their homes and streets with lighted lanterns. In the same way, South Koreans have a popular Lantern Festival organized every November in the enchanting city of Seoul. The colourful lanterns make the city young and seductive as it readies itself to welcome the spirits of ancestors.

From ancient days onward, people have been using lanterns as a source of light. In the Middle Ages, the cities employed watchmen who would go around the streets at night with a lantern in hand. It reduced crimes drastically. Paris was one of the first cities to light up the streets. By the year 1500, most of its public places had

> Human life is in a constant tussle between two forces: of light and of darkness.

street lights. Soon, lanterns were no more a luxury; they became a necessity.

Street lighting gave people better safety and more time for work and fun. It also helped to defeat many fears associated with numerous superstitions.

Fire and light are at the core of every religious tradition. Zoroastrianism believes in Ahura Mazada, the creator of the cosmos. He created two spirits: one is the light of eternal benevolent truth from where flows righteousness, goodness, love and life. The second spirit is that of destruction from where flows darkness, deceit and death. Human life is in a constant tussle between these two forces, between the light and the darkness.

Some ancient cultures viewed death as a voyage from this world to the next. They would place food, wine, money and even an unlit lamp inside the coffin. They hoped that the lamp would give them light in the next world. Excavators at the Roman Catacombs have discovered many lamps used by these ancient cultures.

Light has a significant place in Christianity. Christ is presented as the light of the world. The Holy Spirit descends in the form of fire on the disciples of Jesus and every Christian is called to become a follower of light. Light gives them courage and strength.

The Jewish festival Hanukkah celebrates the festival of lights. It represents the freedom and liberation of Jerusalem. The Muslims, during the festival of Ramadan, light up their homes and mosques with lanterns. For the

Buddhists, light represents enlightenment. The Hindus celebrate Diwali, the festival of light which represents the victory of light over darkness.

A Lantern is useful only if it has a flame. It protects and preserves the small flickering flame inside. We too have a flame in us. This flame is often under the storm. Our wicks are dry and they quench for oil. The flames in us are dying because of our wrong deeds.

Our values, right beliefs and good deeds keep our inner flame alive. Religious scriptures, rituals and traditions ensure this flame is kept alive.

Lantern is a Symbol of Love

A lantern spreads light, life and love. The Holy Bible, like all other sacred books, emphasizes the role of lantern in one's life. Jesus asked his disciples to become a lantern in the world to spread light for those who walk in darkness. "Does anyone ever bring in a lamp and put it under a bowl or under a bed? Doesn't he put it on the lampstand?" he asked. Light is for everyone, not for keeping it hidden. Therefore, the light in us should shine for the benefit of everyone.

Like a lamp on the lampstand, we are to stand out and not hide our light, especially when times are tough. Light will give us the wisdom and courage to stand out, speak up and lift up the lowly. The light inside us should benefit others. This light in us gets reflected through our deeds of selfless love.

It is said that the city of Philadelphia was once known as the 'City of Darkness.' After sunset no one dared to venture out as the streets in pitch dark were ruled by  thugs and robbers. However, Benjamin Franklin, its Post Master General, had an idea. He decided to install a street light at the gate of his house so that people could walk safely at night.

A wealthy man who lived nearby saw this and decided to put up more lights along the streets. Soon the whole city was lit up and thus came the custom of installing street lights in US. The 'City of Darkness' became the city of Philadelphia, meaning the 'City of Brotherly Love'. Light brings life and love.

Are we ready to paint our lives with love that is tender and unconditional, forgiveness that is selfless and sacrificing, trust that is sincere and limitless? If so light your lantern to spread love.

Lantern Offers Choices

The lantern represents choices. We can either light it to live in the light or keep it under a bowl to live in darkness. Once lighted, it conquers darkness. It is strange to note that even in the olden days there were sects and groups who protested against the light. They didn't want light and lanterns. They considered lanterns like today's surveillance cameras infringing on one's privacy, freedom and choice. They chose darkness.

When Covid was sowing the world with the seeds of fear and anxiety and when people feared to come out to help one another, the health workers and the police force were out on the battlefield with fierce determination and immense courage to defeat the havoc caused by it.

When Government asked for volunteers to work in the health sector, not many opted. Annlitta Thomas, my niece, who was entering her first year in college, volunteered to support the cause. When her family objected to her decision, she said, "It's my responsibility as a young student of medicine to help the sick and the needy. If not for this, then why should I pursue this profession?" She had a choice to light the lantern or remain in darkness. She, like many other youngsters, chose to light the lantern.

"I am not bound to win, but I am bound to be true. I am not bound to succeed, but I am bound to live by the light that I have. I must stand with anybody who stands right and stand with him while he is right and part with him when he goes wrong", says Abraham Lincoln.

What do we choose: light or darkness?

Lantern is Other-Centered

A flame loses its life by sacrificing its light for others. It gains nothing except the cheer it spreads around. It flickers, becomes humbler, smaller and finally diminishes by living a life for others. Do we live for others or for ourselves? A lantern is selfless. What about us?

The real hero of Mahabharata, for me, is Karna. He experienced humiliation and lived an ostracized life disowned by his mother and siblings. The Pandavas were jealous of his bravery, benevolence and loyalty. Though he was the son of the Sun god, he lived in darkness ignored by the royalty but loved by the commoners. A son of light exiled to live in the dark!

Arjuna, who was proud of his mastery over archery, felt threatened by the esteem enjoyed by Karna. "Why is Karna loved more than me?" he asked one day to Lord Krishna. Instead of answering, Krishna led Karna and Arjuna to two gold mountains and said, "I shall give one mountain each to each of you, which you must donate to the poor people."

Arjuna immediately went around advertising about the gold mountain and recruited people to distribute the gold to everyone. The villagers were delighted and they started to praise the generosity and goodness of Arjuna. More and more people arrived to receive the gold from Arjuna and he was highly pleased as his fame spread across the country. He admired his own benevolence. He was proud of his charity. He cherished the praises that the villagers bestowed on him.

Krishna then took Arjuna to the other gold mountain that he had gifted to Karna. But they didn't find Karna there. "This gold mountain is all yours. Take whatever you need", he told the villagers and walked away.

Arjuna realized the reason why people loved Karna more than anyone else.

While many of us are proud of our little contributions to make the lives of others, feel good about the praises of others and speak a lot about the good things we have done, the real heroes do the good and just walk away. They don't expect praises or laurels; they shun public displays of honour and recognition; they light the lanterns and live a life for the benefit of others.

Lantern Dispels Darkness

Post-covid workplaces have become alarmingly unhappy, stressed and dissatisfied. I have seen colleagues quitting their well-paid jobs without having a job in hand. "Remaining in this toxic workplace will do me more harm than not having a job", said a colleague when I enquired why he resigned.

> Cliques cause workplaces to become like graveyards where emotionally drained souls wander around.

In my training on 'Demystifying Diversity', I emphasize the importance of nurturing a progressive, harmonious and prosperous team, as many talents quit because of the toxic work culture. They see darkness everywhere with no lanterns to lead them.

Workplaces are becoming poisonous because of the presence of leaders who are greedy, selfish, arrogant and hostile. They create cliques of 'yes men' around them. Such workplaces are characterized by low morale and high politics, low productivity and high attrition. Cliques are suicidal. They cause workplaces to become graveyards where emotionally drained souls wander around.

"Do you know a soul downhearted needing cheer along life's way? If you do, then share your gladness and freely speak kind words today", says Beverly J Anderson, the American Mathematician. Lantern helps to dispel the negativity from our souls. There are so many people who want to come out of darkness. Can we reach out to them and show them the light?

Anthony de Mello in his classic, The Prayer of the Frog, narrates an ancient Japanese practice. The Japanese used to carry paper lanterns in the night as they travelled. The paper shielded a lit candle that was held by bamboo sticks.

A blind man happened to be visiting a friend and since it was late, was offered a lantern to take home with him. "Day and night are the same for me. Why should I need a lantern?" laughed the man. "This lantern is not to lead you home. This is to prevent someone from running into you in the dark", answered his friend.

So the blind man started off with the lantern. It wasn't long before someone crashed into him knocking him down. "You idiot fellow, can't you see the lantern?" lamented the man.

"Brother your candle is out", answered the stranger as he helped the man to get up and walk.

Similarly, many of us carry lanterns but without light. Light your lanterns!

Lantern Represents Progress and Enlightenment

In the Middle Ages, light represented an enlightened society while darkness denoted incivility. Light was a symbol of knowledge, wisdom and progress. Voltaire in his book, 'Siecle de Louis XIV', published in 1751, says, "While five thousand lamps lighted up Paris every night, Rome was not lighted at all." Paris was thought of as a more enlightened society than other cities. Illumination of a city and the enlightenment of humans were two sides of the same coin.

Ancient Greek philosophers like Heraclitus advocated that the world is in constant flux. Soul was conceived as a combination of water and fire. It had to be constantly purified by fire. Indian philosophers named it as enlightenment. Agni was viewed as the bridge between heaven and earth. Because of its immense energy and power, it always remained young.

Fire and light are energy sources. Without them life will perish. Darkness in the world or in the human heart is a sure path to destruction. Likewise the world will perish without light.

Mythologies tell us stories of heroes stealing fire from gods so that humans could live. When god Zeus punished the humans and made the universe dark, the Greek hero Prometheus stole fire from the gods and gave it to them.

Plato interpreted this fire as the light of enlightenment, knowledge, skill, wisdom and goodness. Zeus punished him for his transgression. Prometheus was exiled. He was tied to a huge rock in the desert and eagles were sent to eat his liver. The Greeks believed that the abode of human emotions was the liver.

The eagles would eat his liver during the day but by night his liver would have grown up again only to be eaten again. It showed that knowledge, skill, wisdom and enlightenment could never be destroyed, diminished or defeated. It multiplies. The possessor of light will always be victorious. Light is energy and energy can never be destroyed!

We are people of light. There is a light in each one of us. The light reflects our goodness, truthfulness and values. Those who lead a life of vices live in darkness.

We need to shine our lights brighter to overcome our iniquities.

Lantern Gives Hope

Lantern is like a lighthouse that gives hope, direction and security to those lost in the sea of life. Light is one of the most essential resources that sustains life to thrive in challenging situations.

In many cultures, fire, light and sun represent purity, life and hope. The Indians and the Greeks worshipped the sun god. The ancient Egyptians believed that sun god 'Ra' when opened his eyes, it was day and when he closed his eyes, it became night!

> Lantern is like a lighthouse that gives hope, direction and security to those lost in the sea of life.

Humans discovered fire around 420 million years ago and used it to improve their quality of life. Fire was a sign of hope for a better future. Unlike other animals, they soon learnt the art of using fire to give light, to cook, to warm, to chase off predators, to conquer enemies and to keep insects away. Fire became part of their toolkit. It gave them hope.

I grew up in a home that had no electricity. We would sit around a small pitcher or a lantern to study, eat and pray. We used oil or kerosene to keep the wick burning. My father would hang the lantern on a pole or keep it on a stool to get the maximum light. The light would fill not only the rooms but also our hearts. When I moved on to a hostel that had electric lights, I greatly missed the pleasure of sitting by the dim light of a lantern. Light, big or small, gives hope to everyone.

Lantern Gives Excitement

Our school teachers taught us that matter in an excited state could emanate light. A matter is an amalgamation of its atoms and molecules. When these atoms are charged up, excited and are at high energy, they radiate light in the form of photons.

I believe only those with high energy and excitement can radiate light. Have you experienced the fire in you when you meet people with light? They are like firelighters that can ignite so much energy in you. The more light they emanate, the more energetic they become.

Light symbolizes celebration. Every festival becomes colourful with light. Light gives excitement and fun. It represents good times.

Do we bring excitement, good times and glad tidings to others?

Light Brings Abundance, Prosperity and Wisdom

Many people start auspicious events with the lighting of a lamp. Light symbolises love, charity, abundance, prosperity, well-being and wisdom. Venkat, my friend, once explained to me the meaning of the lamp and the light used in a ceremony.

A cotton wick is placed inside the ghee or oil. The wick represents one's ego that has to be burnt with the fire. The ghee and the oil represent the vices in every person. The fire consumes and purifies these vices. Once the wicks are lit, the lights will go up. This represents our inner self, now purified and without ego ascending to the creator.

"Untruth to truth, darkness to light, death to immortality. Om. Peace", the priest sings the Vedic mantra as he lights the fire.

"A lamp will have up to six wicks and each wick represent a different invocation", says Venkat. One wick is lighted in prayer for normal benefits, two for peace and harmony at home while three are lighted for the blessing of progeny. Four represent all-around prosperity and plenty. Five wicks mean an abundance of wealth and status and six wicks are lighted to gain knowledge and wisdom.

The Parable of Lanterns

Any reflection on light and lantern is incomplete without a glance at the Parable of the Wise Girls that Jesus Christ narrated in the Holy Bible. He was a master storyteller. His parables have captivated millions across the world for the last 2000 years. He used stories to touch the hearts of his followers and thus helped them to live in the new light that emanated from their lanterns.

There were ten girls who took their oil lamps and went out to meet the bridegroom. Five of them were foolish and the other five were wise. The foolish ones took their lamps but did not take any extra oil, while the wise ones took containers full of oil for their lamps. The bridegroom was late in coming, so the girls began to nod and fall asleep.

It was already midnight when the cry rang out, "Here is the bridegroom! Come and meet him!"

The ten girls woke up and trimmed their lamps. Then the foolish ones said to the wise ones, "Let us have some of your oil, because our lamps are going out."

"No, indeed", the wise ones answered, "there is not enough for you and for us. Go to the shop and buy some for yourselves."

So the foolish girls went off to buy some oil; and while they were gone, the bridegroom arrived. The five girls who were ready went in with him to the wedding feast and the door was closed.

The wise girls had the lights lit in their hearts. They were ready with oil too. They were disciplined with values and sound principles and as a result they enjoyed the banquet with the bridegroom. They had prepared well while the foolish were complacent, careless and disrespectful. The wise were full of light while the fools were full of darkness. The wise loved the truth while the fools hated it. The wise clung to love while the fools clung to lethargy.

The wedding festivals in the ancient Middle East were unique. The bridegroom along with his courtier, would travel to the bride's home for the festival. The wedding would last for a week. As the bridegroom would arrive late in the night, it was the duty of the friends of the bride to make sure that the roads and houses were lit up for the guests.

Once the guests arrive, they would walk along with the bridegroom to celebrate the rest of the wedding. They would be ready and waiting for the voice that calls out to them, "Here is the bridegroom! Come out and meet him!"

When they heard this voice, they would trim the wick so that it would burn brightly again. They would also add more oil so that the entire street and houses would become brighter.

In the parable above, we see that though all were given the same instruction, five failed in their duty. They were unprepared. They were like empty lanterns that didn't have light.

All were asleep. However the wise five were awake, watchful and ready with their lanterns on, the moment they heard the announcement. While the other five continued to sleep, the wise decided to wake up and enjoy the dinner.

The foolish five failed to foresee what was imminent. They were complacent and didn't prepare themselves with sufficient oil for the night. They thought they could covet the glory and fame the wise would receive. They did nothing and expected the same treatment as the rest. They postponed their responsibilities and thought they had plenty of time.

Though they knew oil was as essential as the lamp and the wick they carried, they thought of depending on others and failed to prepare themselves. They had the lamp, the wick, the night and the festival. But they missed the oil and as a result, missed the festival too.

We too are sometimes lethargic like these fools! We think we have plenty of time; we think we are superior and pave our way through; we think others are there to help us; we think we can get through with our street smartness.

But our calculations fail and then we blame it on others. We say, 'others are not giving us oil'.

It is also interesting to note that just like the foolish five we too hope for another opportunity and knock on the doors to avail it. However, the reality is strikingly different. There may not be another opportunity at all. We find the doors shut; we discover that we are unprepared; we realize that we have no oil. We expect the door to be open always.

We know in life opportunities don't wait all the time. One must grab it as it passes by. If we miss the opportunity, we live in darkness. Lethargy leads to darkness!

Let Your Light Shine!

"A good deed done by anyone of us in this naughty world can shine like a candle in the middle of the darkest night", says William Shakespeare. So, let us light our lanterns through our good deeds.

> "A good deed done by anyone of us in this naughty world can shine like a candle in the middle of the darkest night."
> William Shakespeare

We saw that light signifies character, values and goodness of a person. These virtues cannot be borrowed but to be cultivated through constant and careful practice and efforts. "Idleness is the workshop of the devil", says Don Bosco, educator and founder of Don Bosco institutions, who lived in the 19th century. Not making sufficient efforts to light one's lantern and not storing enough oil is like giving one's life to the powers of darkness.

An atheist, before his death, willed his large farm to the devil. The village council found it hard to decide on an inheritor for the man. Finally they decided to leave it for the weeds to grow, the house to ruins and the thugs to hide. Soon the farm became a haunted and feared place.

If we don't make conscious efforts to light the lantern, we will soon be ruled by darkness. We must allow the light in us to shine through a virtuous life.

Our words, actions and deeds can be a light for someone. A smile, a word of appreciation, a helping hand or a listening ear may save a life.

A senior HR professional confided to me recently that a death could have been prevented if he was a little more considerate and kind. His colleague came to him for a confidential discussion and he asked him to come on another day as he was in an important meeting. The young man apologized for interrupting and left the room. Unfortunately, that evening he took his life as he was experiencing a deep depression because of a failed marriage.

Everyone is a light for someone, if we choose so.

Were the Wise Really Wise?

Knowledge speaks; wisdom listens. If so, how can we say that the five who had oil in their hands were wise? Were they not selfish and self-centred? They failed to help the needy. Sharing what they had with the other five would soon have left everyone in the dark. Hence they decided to be pragmatic, not wise. They had light in their hands and darkness in their hearts.

While the fools forgot to keep the stock, the wise refused to share the stock. Willing to give freely and share unconditionally is an essential trait of the wise. They were well aware that history will record the takers not the givers.

They were pragmatic, knowledgeable and skilled; but not wise or good. They declined to light the lanterns of others. "Learn to light a candle in the darkest moments of someone's life. Be the light that helps others see; it is what gives life its deepest significance", says Roy T. Bennett, the author of 'The Light in the Heart'.

> "Thousands of candles can be lighted from a single candle and it will never shorten its life by that act of sharing. Happiness, love and kindness never decrease by sharing."
> Buddha

What would have happened if the wise were willing to share the oil? It would have been a positive risk to help the needy. "Thousands of candles can be lighted from a single candle and it will never shorten its life by that act of sharing. Happiness, love and kindness never decrease by sharing", says Buddha. Unfortunately, the wise failed to understand this truth and held on to their light without sharing.

Victor Marie Hugo, the French novelist who lived during the Romantic Movement, influenced many through his novels especially the 'Les Miserables.' It narrates the story of Jean Valjean, a criminal caught for stealing a loaf of bread to feed his nephews and a kind-hearted bishop who transforms Jean Valjean through his act of kindness.

Poverty and extreme injustices experienced by Jean Valjean are portrayed as darkness. One night he reaches the palace of the bishop to steal. But the bishop welcomes him with candles lit and bright. He offers him good food and a warm bed to rest.

Unable to control his habit of stealing, Jean Valjean steals the silver plates of the bishop and runs away into the darkness. However he is soon caught by the police as he tries to sell the plates. They bring him to the bishop and the bishop once again fills the heart of Jean Valjean with light.

He tells the police that Jean is a close friend and that he has given him the silver plates as a gift. "And Jean, you forgot to take the candlesticks", adds the bishop. This act of kindness fills the heart of the convict with light and he becomes a transformed person.

The bishop, unlike the pragmatic girls, was wise. He lends oil, lights the lantern and leads a convict to liberation. He became a lantern for a traveler in darkness.

The Search of Sinope

In the ancient world, there lived a cynic philosopher named Diogenes of Sinope. He would stand in the marketplace with a lantern in his hand and whenever people were passing by, he would hold the lantern onto their faces. When people questioned him, he would say, "I am searching for an honest person." He believed that a person of light is a person of complete truthfulness and transparency in all circumstances.

When his father was exiled from the city of Athens for a defamation case, he accompanied him willingly to take care of him. He would go around begging for sustenance. He rejected all that was not essential for a dignified life like personal possessions and social status.

> "I am searching for an honest person."
>
> Sinope

He believed in self-control and exhorted people to become true to their self. It is said that the only possession he had was a cup that he used for drinking water. But when he saw a little boy drinking water with his hands, he threw the cup away and said, "If that boy can drink water without a cup, so can I".

He revolted against the corrupt political systems of the day through his 'search for an honest person' to expose the double standard of society and the sham of political hypocrisy. He believed that the etiquette, morality and good manners propagated by philosophers were mere lies to hide one's imperfections and falsehood. So he would hold up a lighted lantern on the faces of people in his search for honesty.

His act helped to expose many untruths. Today people hold him in high esteem and revere him as a person who stood for truth.

The Light of the World!

Every person is a 'light of the world'. His benevolence and positivism radiate the world and make him an apostle or a prophet of light. He is like a lighthouse that gives hope and direction, consolation and comfort, safety and security to those in darkness.

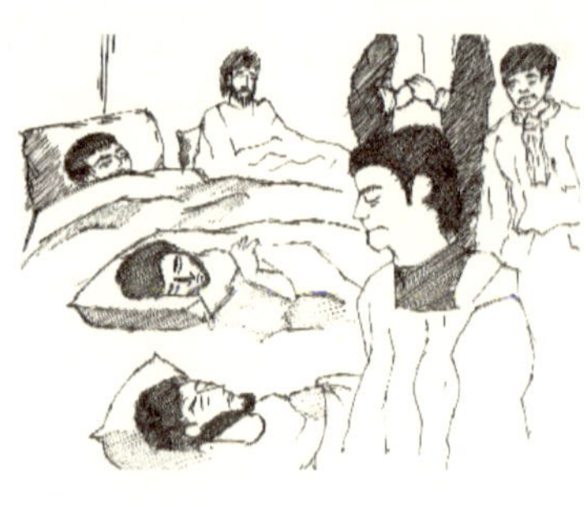

A cholera epidemic ravaged and wiped out 50% of the population of Europe in 1854. Turin in Italy was hard hit. Though the government launched 'lazarettos', make-shift hospitals, to take care of the patients, they found it hard to recruit the staff. Medical staff stayed away because of the fear of infection.

Don Bosco, a renowned educator and social reformer, along with his students, volunteered to combat the disease bravely. He exhorted his team to dedicate their lives to the sick and the needy. He convinced them that if they remained faithful to this noble deed and remained in God's grace, they would be protected and preserved from the epidemic.

He asked his volunteers to follow the recommendations of the health commission strictly. Since sanitizers were not available, he would insist on using vinegar as a sanitizer to minimize the spread of the plague. He trained them to nurse the sick with great devotion.

As he had prophesied, none of his people got infected. They not only took care of the sick but also those orphaned or abandoned due to the pandemic.

He believed in 'amorevolenza', loving-kindness, which later became his educational philosophy. He demonstrated love in action. When the world was in darkness, he became its light.

Similarly, everyone is invited to become a light for others. Be the light!

Just as a lantern is helpful if it gives light, we are humans only if we radiate light. We must be reborn with more love, more compassion, more solidarity, more kindness and more empathy.

The light in us should shine out and illuminate the world to become deeply human and deeply divine.

Light the lanterns! Let your light shine!

References

I am indebted to the following authors for their inspiration.

1. The Speaker's Quote Book by Roy B. Zuck

2. Grow Free Live Free by Dr. Thomas Anchukandam and Dr. Jose Kuttianimattathil

3. The Song of the Bird by Anthony De Mello

4. The Prayer of the Frog by Anthony De Mello

5. The Sower's Seeds Series by Brian Cavanaugh

6. Qualities of a Leader by John C Maxwell

7. Creative Fidelity in Mission by VM Thomas

8. Good to Great by Jim Collins

9. You Can Win by Shiv Khera

10. Pastoral Guide Vol 1 & 2 by Dr. Thomas Pazhayampallil

11. What Got You Here Won't Get You There by Marshall Goldsmith

12. The Road to Hyundai by Kim Myong-Ho

13. The Red Book of Aim Insights by CLHRD

14. He Can Who Thinks He Can by Dr. John Parankimalil

15. Think Like a Monk by Jay Shetty

16. The First 90 Days by Michael D. Watkins

17. New Ideas from Dead Economists by Todd G. Buchholz

18. Never Give Up by Dr. Sajith Cyriac, ssp

19. The Rule of Saint Benedict

20. Atomic Habits by James Clear

21. Jonathan Livingston Seagull by Richard Bach

22. Salt and Light: A Leader on a Pilgrimage by Joshy Thomas

23. Bible references from Good News Bible

https://www.lifehack.org/articles/lifestyle/how-to-find-hope-when-you-are.html

https://www.psychologytoday.com/intl/blog/pieces-mind/201504/finding-hope

https://blog.iqmatrix.com/nurturing-hope

https://godtv.com/its-time-to-cast-your-nets-deeper/#:~:text=You've%20cast%20your%20nets,was%20preparation%20for%20this%20moment.

https://www.psychologytoday.com/intl/blog/kidding-ourselves/201405/the-remarkable-power-hope

https://www.fearlessculture.design/blog-posts/why-pride-is-poison-for-your-soul

https://en.wikipedia.org/wiki/Rat_Park

https://rewardfoundation.org/quitting-porn/three-step-recovery-model/

https://blog.vantagecircle.com/qualities-of-a-good-employee/

https://www.agoodemployee.com/qualities-good-employee/

https://biblehelpsinc.org/publication/qualities-of-a-faithful-christian-worker/

https://www.healthline.com/health/how-to-be-happy#yearly-habits

https://www.inc.com/jeff-haden/10-scientifically-proven-ways-to-be-incredibly-happy-wed.html

https://agastyakapoor.in/2018/06/10/happiness-in-bhagavad-gita/#:~:text=Happiness%2C%20then%2C%20is%20the%20state,permanent%20kind%20%E2%80%94%20that's%20only%20inside

https://www.yourtango.com/experts/dr-susan-heitler-creator-of-power-of-two-marriage/how-save-your-marriage

https://quitpit.com/very-short-stories-with-morals-for-kids/

https://www.verywellmind.com/how-to-boost-your-self-confidence-4163098

https://www.fuckupnights.com/

https://www.zeebiz.com/india/photo-gallery-amitabh-bachchans-career-in-bollywood-now-50-years-strong-113929

https://www.researchgate.net/publication/330620300_Tagore's_Philosophy_of_Religion

https://www.goodreads.com/quotes/21045-if-a-man-is-called-to-be-a-street-sweeper

https:// thefranciscanmethodist.wordpress.com/2018/07/22/sermon-listening-is-an-act-of-love/

https://www.humorthatworks.com/learning/7-types-of-work-relationships/

A Psalm of Life by Henry Wadsworth Longfellow | Poetry Foundation

www.ingramcontent.com/pod-product-compliance
Lightning Source LLC
Chambersburg PA
CBHW031121160726
47989CB00016B/31